Finches

REBECCA K. O'CONNOR

ANIMAL PLANET ♥ PET CARE LIBRARY

Finches
Project Team
Editor: Tom Mazorlig
Copy Editor: Ellen Bingham
Indexer: Ann W. Truesdale
Design concept: Leah Lococo Ltd., Stephanie Krautheim
Design layout: Angela Stanford

T.F.H. Publications
President/CEO: Glen S. Axelrod
Executive Vice President: Mark E. Johnson
Publisher: Christopher T. Reggio
Production Manager: Kathy Bontz

T.F.H. Publications, Inc.
One TFH Plaza
Third and Union Avenues
Neptune City, NJ 07753

Discovery Communications, Inc. Book Development Team
Marjorie Kaplan, President and General Manager, Animal Planet Media
Patrick Gates, President, Discovery Commerce
Elizabeth Bakacs, Vice President, Creative and Merchandising
Sue Perez-Jackson, Director, Licensing
Bridget Stoyko, Designer

09 10 11 12 13   3 5 7 9 8 6 4 2
Printed and bound in Indonesia

Library of Congress Cataloging-in-Publication Data

O'Connor, Rebecca.
  Finches / Rebecca K. O'Connor.
      p. cm. – (Animal Planet pet care library)
  ISBN 978-0-7938-3797-7 (alk. paper)
  1. Finches. I. Title.
  SF473.F5O26 2008
  636.6'862–dc22
                                        2008002326

This book has been published with the intent to provide accurate and authoritative information in regard to the subject matter within. While every reasonable precaution has been taken in preparation of this book, the author and publisher expressly disclaim responsibility for any errors, omissions, or adverse effects arising from the use or application of the information contained herein. The techniques and suggestions are used at the reader's discretion and are not to be considered a substitute for veterinary care. If you suspect a medical problem consult your veterinarian.

The Leader in Responsible Animal Care for Over 50 Years!®

www.tfh.com

Table of Contents

Chapter 1

Why I Adore My
Finch

Finches are one of the most common birds in aviculture and have a long history of being kept for their beauty and lovely vocalizations. The society finch was being bred in China at least 500 years ago. Wealthy members of Victorian Britain once kept finches as status symbols in their homes to liven the décor. Today, bird lovers all over the world keep and breed pet finches for their company as well as their beauty. As scientists and bird fanciers have learned more about the nutritional needs and natural behavior of finches in the wild, more and more species have been captive bred and become readily available.

Although they do not bond to humans like parakeets and parrots do, finches are considered excellent pets by some. They learn to tolerate the presence of people but tend not to like being touched or handled. In fact, finches

prefer the company of other finches rather than that of humans. For some homes, this makes them excellent pets. Although finches require daily care and observation, they don't mind if you go to work and leave them with their pals all day. If you enjoy their vocalizations and watching their interactions, they can be wonderful companions. This book will help you decide if keeping or breeding finches is for you and teach you how to care for them.

What's a Finch?

The word *finch* has come to mean "any variety of small seed-eating birds with a stout bill." All these species of birds have features useful for cracking seeds, such as heavy conical bills, strong skulls, and powerful jaw muscles. The name "finch" has been applied to at least 11 different families and subfamilies of birds around the world, although there is really only one group of "true finches," the taxonomic family Fringillidae. Surprisingly, this family includes the popular canary, which few people would think of as a finch. The other families are Ploceidae, which includes weavers and whydahs; Passeridae; and Estrildidae. The family Estrildidae includes grass and parrot finches as well as nuns, which are the birds that are commonly thought of as pet and aviary finches.

Most finches in aviculture are naturally found in the old world—Africa, Australia, and Asia. They come in a wide variety of colors and sizes, although they are all small birds. Many species have vibrant coloration. It is

Do You Have a Good Finch Home?

Finches don't take up much room, but that doesn't mean they will be happy in the corner of just any home. A little bit of noise and activity isn't a problem. However, a house that is so active that the little birds can't get any peace can be too stressful for finches. If you have cats and dogs and have difficulty convincing them to leave the finches alone, this will also be an issue. Young curious children that continually have their noses and fingers in the finch cage will be hard on finches. Finches require a home that will be attentive to their needs but also give them plenty of peace.

There are dozens of different species that are called finches. All of them are fairly small, seed-eating birds.

quite probably their small size and beautiful plumage that originally encouraged bird fanciers to breed them in captivity.

Some finches have been bred in captivity for so long that they are considered domestic. These finches are relatively easy to keep and breed. They include zebra and society (Bengalese) finches. Other finches less common in aviculture may be more sensitive than these two species. If you wish to keep the more domestic finches, they are likely to thrive as long as they are given a proper environment and nutrition. Other finches will require understanding their natural history, catering to their behavior, and creating an environment as close to their natural habitat as possible. Keeping mixed flocks can be even more challenging, as some species may not get along and can even attack each other and cause injury and death.

Physical Characteristics

Finches weigh from 7 to 30 grams (0.25 to 1 oz; because the birds are so small, grams are normally used to weigh them). Their length is between 3 and 8 inches (20 and 40 cm), and all are considered small birds. They have beaks that are designed for seed husking, although almost all of them eat insects as well.

They are all members of one of four families, but most families include more than a hundred different species. This means, of course, that the variety of finches in the wild is tremendous. However, if you understand their general physical characteristics, you

Lifespan and Aging of Birds

Finches have relatively short lives and tend to live from four to nine years. Their life span depends on their species and—of course—on their care. Finches that get a variety of foods and live in a stress-free environment will live longer than finches that do not get proper care.

Finches have conical beaks adapted for eating seeds. This is a blue-headed cordon bleu finch.

can easily determine if your finch is in good health.

Eyes

Most finches have dark eyes. Their eyes should be round, clear, and shining. Birds with dull-looking eyes or squinted eyelids may be ill. The pupil of the eye should be dark and should not show any opacity. A pale pupil is the sign of an old injury or cataract. There should be no discharge from the eyes or swelling around the eyelids. A finch's eyes should seem alert and aware.

Nostrils

A finch's nostrils are positioned at the beginning of the beak near the top. They are tiny holes that are difficult to see. If you cannot see them from outside the cage, the finch most likely has no problem with them. If you are looking up close, the nostrils should be uniform in size and not show any signs of blockage. If the feathers around the nostrils are matted and there seems to be discharge, the finch may have a respiratory infection.

Beak

The beak of a finch is conical and should be smooth. Depending on the species, the beak is generally gray, black, white, red, or orange. The upper and the lower mandible should always fit together neatly. Beaks that don't fit together correctly can be a sign of injury or a genetic problem.

Overgrown beaks can be a sign of improper feeding.

Ears

The ears on a finch should be difficult to see. They are small holes that are located on the sides of the finch's head. In fully feathered adults, the ears are covered by fine feathers that generally keep them hidden unless the bird is wet. If you can see the ear holes of the bird, it may not be well groomed or may be having a poor molt.

Feet

A finch's feet are tiny, with long, delicate toes, which makes them prone to injury. They should be in perfect condition, without overgrown toenails. Watch that the finch is putting weight on both of its feet and not favoring one, which may indicate an injury. There should be no swelling of the legs or feet or any lumps on the toes, which indicate bumblefoot, a serious health concern. Overgrown toenails and injured feet can be a sign of improper perching. The legs should also not look too scaly, which can be a sign of mites.

Feathers

Although finches come in a variety of feather colorations, their feathers should always look shiny and mostly in excellent condition. They almost always keep their feathers tight against their body unless they are cold. Finches that are consistently fluffed up are most likely ill. Rough, chewed feathering or thin brownish streaks can be

an indication of lice. Bald patches may indicate a skin condition or that another finch is plucking its feathers.

Vent

The vent on a finch is located on the underside at the base of the tail. The vent is used to eliminate waste and to lay eggs. It should be free of debris and, unless the bird is a hen about to lay an egg, should not be swollen. A vent that is crusted with feces or other material may indicate sickness.

Temperament and Behavior

Finches are sensitive birds, and although they can come to feel comfortable around humans, they do not enjoy being scratched or held. It is

A healthy finch has smooth and shiny feathers, as seen on this Lady Gouldian finch.

The zebra finch is the most common finch in American aviculture.

possible to somewhat tame a finch, and there are stories of finches that will ride on their human companion's shoulders, but for the most part, finches prefer their own kind.

A healthy finch will be alert and active. They are busy birds, moving about their enclosure almost constantly. Depending on the species, most finches make peeps and beeps throughout the day. Some finches may sing in the mornings and evenings.

Many other animals prey upon finches in the wild, so they tend to be cautious and wary. If you have an aviary of finches, they will likely move away from you as you approach. Finches will react to predators, like hawks or even your pet dog or cat. They are also likely to be frightened by the introduction of new items into their areas. It is important that you be aware of their sensitive nature and avoid putting too much stress on them.

Finches in the Wild

If you want to be successful at keeping some of the more exotic finches, it is important that you understand how they behave and thrive in the wild. It is best to learn the scientific name

FAMILY-FRIENDLY TIP

A Good Child's Pet?

Finches may be fairly easy to care for and require less interaction than most pets, but that does not necessarily make them the best pet for a child. Finches are sensitive, fragile, and easily killed if their basic care is neglected. They make a wonderful family pet, but the adults in the household should be responsible for their care.

of your finch and then do research. The more information you can find, such as what the species eats in the wild, how it nests, and what sort of habitat it prefers, the more likely it will be that you will have success in keeping a happy, healthy finch. You can start by learning about the different finch families.

Fringillidae, or True Finches

These finches include canaries and are some of the most popular aviary birds. They tend to have a somewhat long tail and peaked head, looking less stocky than other finch species. Many have wing and tail markings that are distinctive, and distinguishable shoulder patches. These finches usually nest in bushes or trees, laying three to five eggs.

Estrildidae

These birds come from Africa, Asia, and Australia and include some of the most beautifully colored birds in aviculture. They include waxbills and munias, grass and parrot finches, and mannikins and nuns. Most thrive in grasslands or brushlands, living in small flocks. They tend to form strong pair bonds. They build unwoven round grass nests with a side entrance, laying four to eight eggs.

Ploceidae

This family includes weavers and whydahs, which are mainly found in Africa and Asia, although some are found in Europe. Female weavers are dull colored, as are males out of breeding season. Whydahs are chestnut or yellow colored and during breeding season have very long tails. In the wild, these birds often breed in colonies, weaving enclosed grass nests that are suspended from branches. They lay two to four eggs.

Passeridae

This is the smallest family of finches, with just over 30 species. They are all small social birds that mainly live in open country. They do not tend to be brightly colored birds, but are mainly brown and gray. They build enclosed nests of grasses, laying two to seven eggs.

Some Common Finches in Aviculture

Zebra Finch

Zebra finches, scientifically named *Teaniopygia guttata castanotis*, are the most common of all finches in American aviculture. They originate from the Australian outback but have

Canaries Are Finches, Too!

Most people think of zebra finches and similar birds when they think of finches. However, it's the canaries that are actually finches. In fact, in scientific terms, they are "true finches" from the only family that is truly a finch. Male canaries of most species are prized singers and are a beloved addition to many homes.

Society finches are very easy to care for, but you should keep them in groups rather than pairs.

been bred for hundreds of years in captivity. They are hardy birds that are about 4 inches (10.2 cm) in length, with zebra-like stripes across their neck and chest and a black-barred tail. Although the zebra finch has been bred for over 30 different color mutations, their normal coloration is brown and gray based. The male has a gray head with chestnut ear patches and a black "teardrop" line below the eyes. A mature male also has a bright red beak. The back and wings are grayish brown, with a white rump patch. The male's chest is finely barred in black and white, his abdomen white, and his sides chestnut colored. The female has a more muted feather coloration than

does the male and a paler beak. Color mutations include white, pied, and fawn variations of this wild coloration.

Zebra finches breed easily and have been studied more than any other finch in captivity. Their quick breeding makes the birds interesting both to genetic scientists and to finch-fanciers wishing to breed for specific traits and colorations. Many of the studies have focused on the finch's song, which is pretty and sung by males generally in the morning. Their other vocalizations are quiet beeps and peeps, and healthy, happy finches vocalize constantly throughout the day.

Zebra finches are readily available and reasonably priced compared with some of the rarer and more sensitive finches in aviculture. Although not every home should necessarily keep finches, zebras are considered a beginner's bird and a good way to investigate the world of finches.

Lady Gouldian Finch

The Gouldian finch (*Erythrura gouldiae*) has been a favorite aviary bird for over 100 years and not just in the United States. The Gouldian finch is popular in the United Kingdom, South Africa, New Zealand, Holland, and Japan. The finch was first bred in Australia before 1886.

This stunning little bird was named after famous explorer John Gould's wife. It is a strikingly beautiful Australian grass finch that comes in three natural color forms: black-headed, red-headed, and yellow-headed, as well as numerous mutations in aviculture.

The Gouldian is approximately 6 inches (15 cm) long. The male in the red-headed form has a scarlet head and nape bordered by a black line. It also may have a black or yellow head. All have a wide turquoise band across the back of the head. The nape and sides of its neck are a light green. The finch's back and wings are a purple-blue. The lower breast, sides of the body, and abdomen are yellow,

fading to white. Hens and immature males look similar to the adult males but with much more muted coloration.

Despite the tremendous number of Gouldian finches bred in captivity, this finch is extremely endangered in its native habitat of northern Australia. Excessive cattle grazing and altered fire regimens are thought to be the cause of the species decline. The finches depend on grasses and seeds, specifically sorghum seeds, and the disruption of the natural growth of these grasses makes it difficult for the species to survive. These finches also eat termites, spiders, and beetles, especially during breeding season.

13

The Expert Knows

Males versus Females

In many species of finch, it is difficult to tell the difference between males and females, but in a few, it is obvious. The condition of having obvious differences between males and females is called sexual dimorphism. In sexually dimorphic finches, males are more brightly colored than are females. In some species, males sing in courtship and become more aggressive. Females generally don't sing, may be less aggressive, and lay eggs (of course!). If you have a male and a female of the same species together, you will most likely get to enjoy the best qualities of both of the sexes.

*Male star finches have bright
red heads; the females lack
this coloration.*

Although the Gouldian can be a
prolific breeder in captivity, it can
be delicate if not kept under the
appropriate conditions. The finches
tend to succumb easily to cold and
damp weather and need to be kept in
sufficiently warm and dry conditions.
They thrive in heat that simulates their
native Australia.

Society (Bengalese) Finch

The society finch (*Lonchura striata*) is
an interesting bird because it has been
domesticated for so long that there is
no population of this bird in the wild.

It is perhaps the domesticated version
of the white-backed munia, evolved
from a Chinese subspecies that was
imported to Japan several hundred
years ago. Selective breeding of this
species resulted in the society finch
and its variety of mutations that are so
popular today.

The society finch is about 4 inches
(10.2 cm) long. No two society
finches look alike, and there are three
basic colorations. They are brown
mottled, yellow mottled, or white. Even
within these colorations, the shade,
distribution, and intensity of these

colors varies greatly. Males and females look similar, but only the male sings and will do so during breeding season.

The society finch is an excellent breeder and probably the easiest of the finches to keep. They are hardy birds and, as long as they are given proper care, will thrive. Unlike most finches, they breed better in a cage than in an aviary. The finches are almost too social, gathering and interfering with one another's nesting. Pairs should be separated for breeding. However, at all other times, this highly social bird should be housed in groups.

Cordon Bleu

There are three species of cordon bleu, all sharing a beautiful pale blue body that has won many people over to the world of breeding finches. This shade of blue is unusual in finches, and many finch fanciers find it appealing. They are types of African waxbill that come from the savannahs, dry forests, and hedges outside of villages. They tend to live in pairs and inhabit thornbushes.

The cordon bleu is 4.75 inches (12 cm) long. In the red-cheeked cordon bleu (*Uraeginthus bengalus*), the male has brown wings and back with blue sides, breast, and head. They have a bright red patch over the ear. The female is missing this red patch and has paler coloring. The other two species are the Angolan cordon bleu (*U. angolensis*), which has similar coloration but is missing the red patch, and the blue-headed cordon bleu (*U. cyanocephala*). This

finch can be distinguished by its blue crown. All three species are closely related, with nearly identical requirements in captivity.

Although the cordon bleu is a popular finch, it is delicate. They can be extremely sensitive to the cold, and keepers must take care in acclimating them and keeping them in the appropriate temperature. With proper care, they are reliable breeders and remain bonded all year. They fit well

Do You Need a Pair?

It is not true that a single finch will die of loneliness. However, a life with another finch is a much nicer one. Finches don't become as tame as parrots can and will not bond with you like many other pets will. They will learn to recognize you and perhaps even interact with you, but they will always prefer other finches for company. If you are going to have one finch, you should probably have two. Your finches will appreciate the feathered company, and you will enjoy watching them interact.

into mixed aviaries, but during breeding season, only one pair at a time should be in an aviary. The males can become aggressive with one another.

Star Finch

The star finch (*Neochmia ruficauda*) is one of the most popular Australian finches for both beginners and experts. They are found in northern Australia and live in reeds and tall grasses along rivers and streams. They live in flocks except during the breeding season, when they break into pairs.

The star finch is 4.5 inches (11.4 cm) long. The male's head and upper throat is red, with white spots around the throat and over the ears. The beak is red. Its wings are grayish brown and its upper sides grayish green to olive. The belly is yellowish-white. The upper tail feathers are red. Females are more muted than males. There are three mutations in star finches: yellow, fawn, and pied.

The star finch lives well in mixed aviaries with finches of similar size, and multiple breeding pairs can share territory if there is plenty of foliage in the aviary. They can be put into outdoor aviaries but can be sensitive to the cold and need shelter from cold and wet weather even in the summer.

Spice Finch

The spice finch (*Lonchura punctulata*) is also called the scaly-breasted munia. It is a fairly common finch species and is readily available in the United States. There are 12 subspecies of the finch in Asia, where the species is native. Originally, the finch traveled to Europe on spice ships, which is where the hearty bird got its name.

They are 4.5 to 4.75 inches (11.4 to 12 cm) long, with a black beak and reddish chocolate-brown head, neck, and upper breast. The lower breast and flank are white, with black scale markings. The sexes are similar and difficult to tell apart, but only the males

Taming Finches

Since finches prefer other finches, rather than people, for company, it can be much harder to train them than other birds. However, it isn't impossible. You can teach your finch to trust you and maybe even fly to your finger if you are patient and spend a great deal of time with her. You will have to spend a lot of time near the cage, sitting quietly to start with so that the finch learns not to worry about your presence. Then you can begin to offer her treats. Eventually you may even be able to get her to sit on your finger. If you don't want to put in all this effort, don't worry. You can still enjoy your finches from a short distance.

sing. Immature birds lack the darker head and have uniform buff underparts.

Juveniles are light brown above, paler below, and a shade darker on the breast and flanks; they lack any markings.

The spice finch feeds mainly on seeds and grasses as well as cultivated rice where available in the wild. They breed in colonies where abundant, sometimes with the nests touching one another. The hens lay three to seven eggs. Although they are not exceedingly difficult to care for, spice finches are difficult to breed.

Chapter 2

The Stuff of
Everyday Life

Although finches appear to be easier birds to care for than most, the requirements for keeping healthy, happy finches might be more than you expect. It is not enough to throw some seeds into a bowl and forget about your finches. They deserve the best care possible, and this chapter will explain the sorts of housing and accesories you will need for giving them that care.

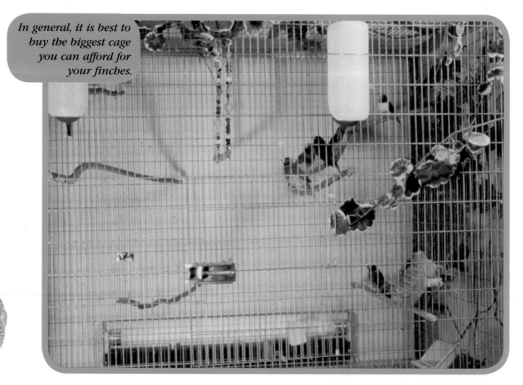

In general, it is best to buy the biggest cage you can afford for your finches.

The most important thing you need to decide on and arrange before your new finches come home is housing. As with all birds, basically, the bigger the cage is, the better. However, you are probably limited by where you live and how much room you have to give to the birds. You may also have financial considerations. It will be far more expensive to build an aviary than to buy a single cage. Consider the possibilities and then give your finch the best new home you can.

Indoor Cage

If you plan on having only a couple of finches, an indoor cage can do the trick. There is a vast number of styles to choose from, however, and you'll want to have some idea before you start shopping. Decide what your budget will be and how important it is to you that the cage match the décor of your home. Regardless of what cage you choose, make sure that it is one that is safe and secure for finches.

Cage Purpose

Finch cages can be used for different purposes. There are exhibition cages, stock cages, and fancy cages that are meant to look nice in the home. Exhibition cages are smaller and meant only for displaying birds in show situations. However, they are excellent for transporting birds, so if you think you will be moving your finches around, exhibition cages are nice to have handy. Stock cages are often used in bird rooms by serious finch breeders who wish to separate out specific pairs for breeding.

Stock cages are not fancy but work well for housing finches. They can be made or purchased and are frequently unpainted wood with removable sliding panels for separating birds. For easy cleaning, the wood should be painted with nonlead paint before using. These cages can also be purchased in tiers for keeping multiple birds. Another possibility for stock caging is metal panels, which allow you to build your own cage. You can assemble the paneling into the most appropriate size for the area you have available.

Cage Size

As stated above, the bigger the cage is, the better. Although you will see that many of the cages labeled for finches in pet stores are tiny, you will have healthier, more active finches if you give them a much bigger cage. Get a cage that is at least 20 inches (50.8 cm) long. Cages that have balconies, sloping sides, and pointed roofs are attractive, but they are not the best arrangement for finches. The birds require more open area for flying, so they can injure themselves in corners.

The cage should be longer than it is high, leaving plenty of open space for zipping back and forth in the cage. The bars of the cage should be spaced specifically for finches, with the bars

at half an inch (1.3 cm) apart. Wider spacing could allow finches to escape or, worse, to get caught between the bars, injuring or even killing themselves.

Cage Materials

Unlike parakeets and other small parrots, finches do not chew cage materials, so there is a wide variety of caging available. Wood cages can work well as long as they are painted with lead-free paint. Plastic and metal cages are also good choices, as long as the metal is nontoxic. Avoid brass, which is poisonous, and galvanized wire, which can be responsible for zinc toxicity in birds. A good choice is stainless steel, which is attractive, easy to clean, and inexpensive.

FAMILY-FRIENDLY TIP

Caring Kids

It is a wonderful idea to involve your children in caring for finches. There is much to learn in their care. Patience, responsibility, and a wonder for living things are just a few of the things a child might learn. However, children should be supervised and never be the sole caregivers to the finches. It takes only a few days of forgetting to feed the tiny creatures to kill them.

Metal finch cages are durable and easy to clean, but do not buy one made of galvanized wire, which is toxic to birds.

Cage Features

Something to keep in mind when looking at cage features is the ability of quick and small finches to escape. Cages with removable bottom trays for easy cleaning should have flaps that close when you pull out the trays so that finches cannot escape. Sliding doors that open and close easily should be conveniently placed to make changing bowls and perches easy without disturbing the birds.

Avoid cages with scrollwork or other ornate features in which a finch could get a toe caught. Also watch out for sharp edges or any other features that could be dangerous to the bird. Simply designed cages with features that allow easy access for cleaning and care make the best choices.

Cage Placement

It is a good idea to purchase a cage that can be easily moved. Finches need sunlight, so keeping the cage near a sunny window that isn't drafty is an excellent idea. However, in the warmer months, moving the cage onto a patio or some other safe and sunny place is wonderful for finches as well. Sunlight is an important factor in the health and well-being of the little birds. Just make sure that the cage is protected from direct sunlight and that some part of the cage remains in the shade.

Finches can be timid, so it's a good idea to choose a location for the cage that isn't too busy. Some traffic is fine, but your finches probably won't be comfortable if they are right in the middle of a big dinner party. It is best to keep them out of the kitchen as well. Fumes and smoke from cooking and cleaning can be dangerous to sensitive small birds. Also make sure that wherever the cage is placed, it is safe from dogs, cats, and other pets that could be dangerous to the birds.

Indoor Aviary

Another option for indoor finches is an aviary. If you have the room to place an aviary inside, it can be an excellent housing choice. A larger aviary will give finches the opportunity to fly and get plenty of exercise. A well-designed indoor aviary can also add attractive and lively décor to your home.

Size

How big your indoor aviary is will most likely depend on the space you have available. The longer the aviary is, the more opportunity finches will have to fly. Although finches will fly up and down in a higher aviary, they are more likely to get flight exercise flying lengthwise. Choose an aviary that is as long as you can make it if you are building your own. Some pet suppliers also sell nice premade aviaries that are meant to be used indoors. It is helpful to choose an aviary that stands 3 feet (0.9 m) above the floor so that the finches are easily viewed and enjoyed.

Materials

A good indoor aviary will be constructed of a wood or metal frame and fine wire mesh. Some aviaries are made with Plexiglas sides, which keep seeds from scattering on the floor. However, Plexiglas sides will mean less circulation of air, and they can also be difficult to clean. If you build your own indoor aviary, you can paint the wood to match your home and choose vinyl-coated mesh that matches, as well.

Finches With Other Pets

Dogs and cats are dangerous to finches—so are ferrets, snakes, and many other common pets. Make sure you keep finch cages out of reach of other household pets. Do not trust them alone in the same room. Even pets that are just curious can terrify finches and cause them to injure themselves. Also be careful of finch escapes. If your finches get out of their cage, they could be quickly snapped up or injured by other animals in the house.

Features

Your aviary should be constructed so that you can easily change bowls and clean without any finches escaping. If the aviary floor is accessible to the birds, it should be washable and can be lined with newspaper. In a roomy aviary, it is a great idea to add potted nontoxic plants and natural perches. The inhabitants of the aviary will also appreciate a place to bathe.

Placement

The aviary should not be placed in the middle of a room. The birds will be nervous if they can be approached from all sides and won't feel comfortable in their cage no matter

how big it is. The best choice is a bright and draft-free corner. You can even paint a landscape scene on the wall behind the aviary if you wish to add a little extra charm to the room.

Bird Room

If you have a large home and an even larger fondness of finches, you can consider converting an entire room into a bird room. The room should have cleanable floors and be painted rather than have wallpaper. It should be free of any furniture or anything else that isn't specifically in the room for the finches. The room should be dry, easy to clean, and easy to air out as well. Any windows should have

An indoor aviary allows you to keep a flock of finches. This one houses spice finches, society finches, and others.

frosted glass or mesh in front of them to prevent finches from injuring themselves by mistakingly flying into the glass to get outside.

It is helpful if windows are screened and can be opened to allow fresh air and sunlight into the room on warmer days. Windows could also lead to an outdoor aviary where birds can get outside for sun and fresh air in good weather.

Treat the room much as you would an aviary. Make sure there are plenty of branches and perches but not so many that flying is restricted. Potted nontoxic plants can be added in the room. The bird room can also be divided if you are breeding species that need to be separated from one another.

Furnishing and Accessories

Once you've decided how to house your finches, it's important that you set up the cage appropriately. You will need to make sure that the birds are able to get exercise, easily get to food and water, and remain as safe as possible inside their enclosure.

Perches

Choosing perches and placing them appropriately is one of the most important aspects of your finches' habitat. Birds spend a tremendous amount of time on their feet, and any injuries to their feet can take a long time to heal.

Perches should be thick enough that the finches can wear down their toenails, which tend to grow quickly. A variety of thicknesses can be used for

Do Finches Need Toys?

Finches will not play with most parrot toys, but there is no reason not to offer finches suitable toys as long as you don't clutter their cage. They might even have a little bit of fun, if only to explore the new additions to their cage. Try bells, small ladders, and swings.

an aviary that has different species of different sizes. Natural perches are an excellent choice because they are of naturally varying thicknesses. Generally, perches for most finches should be no thicker than 3/8 to ½ inch (1 to 1.2 cm) wide.

Plastic perches should be avoided if they are slick, which will make them difficult for the birds to grasp. Wooden dowels can also be used if they are of an appropriate size, but it may be a good idea to roughen the surface with coarse sandpaper. Avoid any perches that are hollow and might make good homes to mites, lice, and other parasites.

Concrete perches are a possibility, but having nothing but concrete to perch on can be hard on finch feet. It is also not a good idea to use the sandpaper sheaths made to fit over wooden dowels. These too are hard on the birds' feet. They tend to get damp, harbor bacteria, and become easily soiled.

Rope perches are also available, and although they look nice as well as comfortable, they can be problematic.

Offer your finches perches in a variety of materials and diameters to help keep their feet healthy.

Loose string can be dangerous to finches. They can get their head caught in a loop of string and be strangled or even just catch a toe and injure themselves. If you must use rope perches, be sure to trim any excess string away.

Place perches so that birds can perch without hitting their wings or tail on the side walls or wire mesh when sitting. Take care to not place them over food and water bowls as well, so that the birds do not defecate in their food and water. The perches should also be placed so that plenty of flying room remains available for the birds. Don't overdo the number of perches in a cage or aviary, creating clutter. Four or five perches in a cage are sufficient.

Be sure to attach perches securely. Falling perches can be dangerous to finches, and perches that wobble can be uncomfortable for the birds, making them uneasy. Wooden perches can be secured with screws and a washer in aviaries that are mainly wire mesh. They can also be whittled down and notched, then squeezed into place.

There are a variety of ways to secure perches; just make sure that they are stable once placed.

Substrate

The best substrate to use for the bottom of indoor cages is newspaper. It is nontoxic, is easy to clean up, and allows you to easily see leftover food and droppings. You'll be able to monitor both your birds' health and their eating habits if you use newspaper in the cage. Outdoor caging can have different substrate, but overall it is important that the floor of the cage or aviary is easy to clean and does not encourage the growth of bacteria and mold. Corncob bedding, walnut shells, and wood shavings can retain moisture and cause problems with mold and bacteria, which may ultimately affect the health of your bird.

Dishes, Cups, and Bowls

There are a variety of bowls and cups that can be used for drinking, eating, and bathing. Pet stores offer a large selection, and you'll need to choose a few different ones for your finches. Even if you have only a pair of birds, you'll need more than just one dish for seeds and one for water.

Plastic is the least desirable choice for bowls. Although plastic bowls and cups are durable and inexpensive, they easily harbor bacteria and are difficult to thoroughly clean. Ceramic bowls are a good choice, but stainless steel ones are even better. Both are durable and easy to clean, but the stainless steel is nearly indestructible and will last longer than any other choice.

If you have a pair of finches, you may want to get an automatic feeding bowl. Make sure you choose one with a wide mouth; that way, seeds will be less likely to get stopped up in the hole. Be sure to check automatic feeders carefully and daily. A bowl full of husks may look like it is full of food, and you should tap the feeder to check that food is dropping into the bowl.

If you choose bowls that have a hood on them to prevent your finches from flinging food about, be sure to check that your finch is actually

eating. This is true of any new bowl that you put in the cage. A nervous bird may starve rather than eat from a bowl that she perceives as dangerous. So make sure that you see your finches eating and drinking.

All the smaller bowls have clips and rings that will allow you to attach them to the cage. Be sure to place bowls near to perches where birds can access their food easily. You'll need to clean seed bowls periodically and clean out water and fresh food bowls daily. You may want to get two sets of bowls so that they can be swapped easily for cleaning.

If you have a large group of finches of different species, you may need to get large open bowls for feeding on the ground. Some finches forage for food naturally on the ground and prefer eating that way. You can also supply different types of

Natural branches make excellent, inexpensive perches for finches.

seeds in individual bowls. If you have numerous birds, this can save seed waste. If you feed a seed mix, finches tend to scatter the seeds that don't appeal to them and waste them.

A ceramic or stainless steel bowl should also be left out for bathing. It should be a shallow dish of water that the birds would be unlikely to drown in. Bathing dishes should be changed daily, because the birds will drink out of them. These dishes of water on the ground are likely to collect debris and quickly become soiled. Again, having an extra to swap is a good time-saving idea.

Seed Catchers

If you have finches in a cage indoors, you may want to put a seed catcher on the cage. Some cages come with skirts that catch fallen seeds before they hit the floor. You can put up your own acrylic guards around the bottom half of the cage or secure a cloth "bloomer" around the base of the cage to stop some of the seed scatter. However, it won't stop all of the seeds. Remember that part of the finch's job in the wild is to scatter seeds. A happy finch will most likely get seeds and seed hulls on your floor. Invest in a good vacuum cleaner!

Cage Covers

Cage covers can be helpful if you have new finches that are nervous or you want your finches to get a little extra sleep. You can purchase premade covers that are meant to fit your cage specifically. You can also make your own. If you aren't good at sewing and don't have a seamstress in your home, a piece of dark fabric or a sheet can work just fine. Take care that it doesn't have frayed edges or loose strings. Finches searching for nesting material can get tangled in the thread and injure themselves.

Lighting

Lighting is an incredibly important aspect of finch care, especially if you plan on breeding your finches. Length of day is a critical factor in giving finches time to eat enough to maintain the energy required to raise a brood of chicks. Natural light is also a means of generating essential vitamins and overall well-being. Some finches will not come into their full colors unless they have enough natural light.

If your birds live primarily indoors, you can supplement their lighting by giving them full-spectrum light from a bird lamp. Full-spectrum bulbs and fluorescent lights that are made for plants and reptiles can be used to give finches some extra sunshine. Shine the light on the cage, but make sure that it doesn't make the cage too hot.

Heaters

Most finches are exotic birds from warm climates and require warm temperatures. Many thrive at temperatures between 65° and 70°F (18° and 21°C) and some, like the Gouldian finch, require even warmer temperatures of 68° to 86°F (20° to 30°C). If your home gets below 65°F (18°C) in the winter,

Some finches prefer to roost in a nest box even when they aren't breeding.

Busy Birds Are Happy Birds

Finches should have something to do all day. Interacting with one another, foraging through a variety of food, building a nest, and exploring new perches and branches will keep them busy. The busier they are, the happier they will be.

you may need to give even indoor finches supplemental heat such as covered heaters or heat lamps. Finches can easily become ill or die if temperatures get too low for them.

Nest Boxes

Some species of finches prefer to sleep in nest boxes. So even if you are not breeding them, you may want to supply them with boxes to sleep in. Different species prefer different sorts of nests, so you will want to research to discover what will work best with your bird. Many finches prefer a wicker-type nest. Other finches may be happier in a semi-open box or an enclosed nesting box.

Natural Fun

Unlike parrots, parakeets, and cockatiels, finches don't really play with toys. However, that doesn't mean that you

shouldn't equip their cages in such a way that they are busy and entertained. The best thing you can do for your finches is to set up an environment that is as close to their natural habitat as possible.

Finches spend a tremendous portion of their day foraging for food and eating. Their tiny little bodies burn large amounts of energy, and with such high metabolism, they eat nearly all day. You can help them simulate this natural behavior by giving them a large variety of food and presenting foods in natural ways. Potted nontoxic plants or aviaries with plantings can add to a natural environment. Grasses that produce edible seeds can give finches a natural means of foraging. Putting reeds in the enclosure for finches that are found in areas that naturally have reeds can simulate their natural environment. You can do this by tying bunches of reeds together and leaning them up against a corner. Consider not only the plants that will add to their habitat, but also their natural behaviors.

Finches that are colony breeders will be happiest in colonies. You will see more natural behavior as the

Giving your finches (Java sparrows in this photo) edible branches or grasses lets them perform natural foraging behaviors.

Overcrowding

Keeping too many birds in your cage or aviary is an easy way to instantly have cleaning issues. Perches, bowls, and the entire environment will get dirty so quickly that you won't be able to keep up. Overcrowded cages are not only dirty but dangerous. Birds can easily get ill and may even get aggressive with one another. Disease is easily spread from feces-contaminated water and food. Also, weaker birds may have a difficult time getting to the food and water they need, easily becoming ill and even dying. Never keep more birds than the enclosure can reasonably hold or you will have trouble maintaining your flock.

finches interact with one another. Providing them with nest boxes and nesting materials will keep them occupied. You may enjoy watching the courting behavior of males and even the nest building. All these activities are natural and keep finches active. Whichever species you choose for pets, the best way to keep them well-adjusted and fit is to simulate a natural environment.

Hospital Cages

Even if you keep your finches in an aviary, you should still have a smaller cage to quarantine new or sick birds. If a bird gets ill, you don't want to be scrambling to set up a good place to keep her. It's better to have a cage prepared for emergencies. It is also important that this cage be somewhere away from the other finches. If your new finch or your sick finch turns out to be contagious, you could lose your whole flock.

A quarantine cage can be smaller and should be rectangular, preferably with three solid sides and a grated front. This way you can easily keep the cage warm but not allow it to overheat. A sick bird will need to stay warm. The cage should also have a tray that slides out. This way you can line the cage with newspaper and keep an eye on the bird's droppings. This will allow you to watch a new bird for any signs of illness and note any changes in a sick bird.

Outdoor Aviaries

Now that we have looked at all the options for indoor housing, we should investigate outdoor aviaries. Having an outdoor home for finches can be far more expensive and time-consuming, but even if you start with a pair of birds indoors, you may find that you catch the "finch bug" and want to breed and keep larger flocks. Building an outdoor aviary can be not only a fun way to enjoy finches but also an impressive addition to your landscape. It is quite possibly the best way to keep finches.

If your aviary is attached to your house, it will be easy to access and to clean.

Choosing the Aviary Site

The first thing that you will want to consider when building an outdoor aviary is location. There are many things to consider in the ideal location of an aviary. The most obvious one is space. Many finch fanciers find that they add on to their first aviary, so it is a good idea to choose an area of your yard with ample room.

Another consideration is the proximity to your house. You'll want to be able to get to the aviary easily, so that it isn't too difficult to get to your birds for daily feedings as well as to check on them. If they are close enough to the house, you might be able to hear if there is a problem with your flock. Proximity will also give you easier access to electricity and water.

Give some thought to shade and sunlight in the location that you choose. Trees are great for shade, but trees that hang over the aviary can be a nuisance. They will drop leaves in the aviary, making cleanup even more problematic and encouraging wild birds to perch over your aviary, contaminating it with their droppings. However, protection from wind and rain is important, and surrounding trees or shrubs can provide some defense. A location that receives morning sunlight is also great for birds.

Consider the activity level around the site of the aviary as well as its security. It is a good idea to have your aviary positioned somewhere that is unlikely to be vandalized. However, it is not a good idea to build the aviary right in the middle of your family's play area. Finches need some seclusion to feel comfortable and to be encouraged to breed.

Buying or Building

The next thing you will need to decide is how you are going to construct your outdoor aviary. There are many companies that make prefabricated aviaries. You can check with aviary suppliers and compare prices and products to find what will best suit your needs. Of course, the drawback to buying a premade aviary is that you most likely will not be able to design it to suit exactly what you need or want. Whether you decide to buy an aviary or build one from scratch, you will need to consider two features of the aviary, the shelter and the flight cage.

The Shelter

The shelter is a place where the finches can retreat to sleep at night or when the weather is bad. It can be a simple construction but needs to be solid all around to allow for easy heating and to keep the inside dry. However, having some windows covered by mesh can be helpful in summer when the room heats up and for added circulation. In hotter climates, finches may retreat inside to the shelter if it gets too hot outside. The shelter should be a place that is always comfortable no matter what the weather.

The shelter is connected to an outdoor flight and can be set up so that it is easily closed off from the flight when necessary. The shelter should have entries with hinged landing platforms that can be closed. This is basically an indoor flight. In areas with harsh winters, this building will need to be more solid and easily heated all winter.

The Flight Cage

The flight cage can be constructed from panels made by a wood frame and wire mesh. All three sides connecting to the shelter should be open, allowing fresh air and sunlight into the flight. You may also want to put a false roof of a second layer of wire mesh so that cats, birds of prey, and other predators cannot get to finches hanging from the wire of the roof. The flight cage will likely be where the birds spend the

Lost Birds

If you lose a finch outside, chances are you won't get it back. Getting lost outside is pretty much a death sentence for these little birds. If your lost finch is still around and has a mate, you can put the cage outside and see if the finch will come back to land on top of it. If so, you can try to trap the wayward bird. A box propped up on a stick with a string tied to the stick works quite well.

majority of their time if you live in an area that has mild weather.

Aviary Floor

It is best if the aviary floor is not dirt unless it is going to be heavily planted. Dirt floors are difficult to keep clean and will quickly saturate with droppings and cast-off food. Gravel can be a good floor substrate if it is hosed and raked weekly. The flight cage can also be planted with turf and hosed. However, the best choice for both the flight and the shelter is probably concrete.

Concrete is easily cleaned and dries quickly. A concrete floor will also inhibit rats and other pests from burrowing into the aviary and causing problems. Just be sure that when you lay the concrete, you give it a gentle slope so that it drains appropriately.

Safety Porch

A safety porch is an important addition to any aviary. Finches easily escape if you enter the aviary directly. It is another expense to add a safety porch but definitely a worthwhile investment.

The safety porch can be as small as a 3-foot by 3-foot (0.9 m) square enclosed area that you enter, closing the door behind you before opening the aviary door. It doesn't need to be solid; a frame with wire mesh will work fine. The idea is to catch any finches that happen to fly out of the flight, before they make it outside.

When you construct the safety porch, take some care in the way the

The Expert Knows

Safe Plants for an Aviary

When planting your aviary, you will want to choose plants that thrive in your climate. More important, choose plants that are safe for the birds. Here are a few safe choices:

Bamboo

Blackberry

Clematis

Conifer (dwarf pine)

Dog rose

Grass

Honysuckle

Raspberry

doors are hinged. Just be sure that the outer door opens outwardly and the door entering the flight opens inwardly. This will make carrying items in and out of the flight easier.

Plantings

You may want to seek assistance when planning for the addition of plants in your aviary. You'll want to find out what plants are nontoxic and appealing to the species of finches you plan to house. You will also want to know what plants are suitable to the climate you live in.

When drawing up your plans, consider how quickly the plants will get to be the full size they will grow. You will still need to get into the flight to check on birds that look ill and maybe on occasion to check a nest, so you will want enough room to maneuver in the flight.

Plant started shrubs and other greenery rather than planting seeds. Some seeds are treated and poisonous, and it is possible that the finches might consume them. If you grow vines and trailing plants, set up trellises for them inside the aviary. If they grow up the wire mesh, they will likely block out sun and damage the fine wires. Trellises will also give finches extra perching.

Water Features

If you have a particularly spacious flight, you can consider adding water features to your aviary. The sound of flowing water is just as appealing as the finch chatter, adding beauty and ambience. However, you'll want to take care that the water features are shallow, so that young birds don't accidentally drown.

You'll need a source of electricity if you put in a water feature. The

This aviary has two highly recommended features: a concrete floor and a safety porch.

Aviary finches will enjoy a birdbath or other water feature, as these Lady Gouldian and owl finches are doing.

electricity will run the pump that keeps the water moving. Stagnant water can cause harmful bacteria to grow and be dangerous to the birds. Make sure that the feature has a gradient as well to ensure good water flow. You may also need to periodically clean the area thoroughly.

You can easily find prefabricated units and liners at pet stores and home improvement centers. When you design your water feature, take care that there are no steep sides. Coarse gravel and large stones can also be added so that the water is never too deep and birds looking for a drink find firm footing.

Breeding Room

If you get heavily involved in breeding finches, you may need a room dedicated to individual cages for your birds. Some finches breed better when separated from the flock. If you are wishing to breed for particular characteristics, you will need to handpick pairs and set them up together. Otherwise, your breeding pairs will be random. There are also some species of finches that become so aggressive in an aviary when they breed that they can be dangerous to the other birds.

A dedicated breeding room will likely have a wall of cages, running water, and a source of heat. This could be inside your home or attached to your aviary. This sort of room isn't entirely necessary though. If you are breeding society finches or zebra finches, you may not need anything other than a suitable outdoor aviary. Keep in mind that if your finch hobby turns to more difficult breeds or to showing, you'll want a breeding room.

The Stuff of Everyday Life

Cleaning House

Keep a schedule for cleaning your finch cages, and your finches will be more likely to stay healthy. However, you need to be careful about which cleanser you use.

Never use household cleansers. They contain chemicals that can be deadly to your bird. Here are some good choices for cleaning products:

- Soap and hot water is a perfect cleaner for daily use.
- A 10-percent bleach solution mixed with water is a great disinfectant. Just be sure to rinse well after disinfecting.
- Grape seed extract makes a wonderful safe disinfectant. You can purchase it from health food stores and bird supply stores.

Predators

In an outdoor aviary, predators can pose a real problem to finches. A predator outside of the cage can frighten finches and cause them to fly back and forth erratically, possibly injuring themselves. Frantic finches can also be easy to grab and pull through the mesh. Snakes and rats can find their way into the aviary and eat chicks and eggs.

It is important to do the best you can to seal off the aviary from potential predators. A cement foundation and a reinforced skirt around the bottom of the aviary can make a difference. Having well-behaved dogs in the yard can also discourage predators from trying to make a meal out of your birds. If you live in a more rural area, you might even try adding some guinea fowl to your yard. Guinea fowl will stay busy all night keeping cats and other predators out of the yard, inadvertently keeping your finches safe. However, they may wander into a neighbor's yard and can be quite noisy. The best defense may be to keep your aviary battened down and impossible for predators to penetrate.

Keeping it Clean

Regardless of whether you keep your finches inside in a cage for two or outside in a large aviary, keeping healthy birds requires keeping a clean cage. You'll want to make a schedule for cleaning and disinfecting and stick to it. The cleaner your finches' housing is, the less likely you will have diseases in your flock.

Caring for finches takes quite a bit of work. There are tasks that should be done daily, weekly, and monthly. Every day, the food and water dishes should be washed out with soap and hot water. Seeds should be checked and changed if they are not fresh. In cages, papers or other substrate should be changed. Take the opportunity to inspect the newspaper when you change it to make sure the droppings look normal.

Every week, the whole cage should be cleaned. Wash the cage tray with soap and hot water and dry it before putting it back into the cage. Wipe down any soiled branches and perches. If the cage bars are dirty, clean them as well. Take care that you do not terrorize the finches inside the cage. Move slowly and back off if they are thrashing around in the cage. In outdoor aviaries, the ground should be raked and any gravel or concrete washed down.

Once a month, everything should be thoroughly cleaned. In outdoor aviaries, the floor should be scrubbed and disinfected with a mild solution of bleach, preferably when the birds are locked out of the area that you are cleaning. All bowls and dishes should also be disinfected with bleach. Nest boxes that are not currently in use should be cleaned out. Perches can be scrubbed and then heated in the oven at 200°F (93.3°C) for 45 minutes. This will dry out the wood, kill any parasites, and disinfect the perch.

Storing Food

An important consideration for keeping your finches' area clean and parasite-free is carefully storing seeds and other foods. Rats love eating seeds and are not only dangerous but carry a variety of diseases. Store seeds in airtight containers. Metal containers are best, because rats can easily chew into plastic containers. Keeping

an outdoor aviary clean and cleaning up excess seeds can also keep rats from running rampant around your finches. Eliminate their food source, and you should have an easier time keeping rats out of your aviary.

Another problem with seeds is moths. If you have tiny moths flying around your home, chances are they are coming from your seeds. If you have small amounts of seed, you can easily solve this problem. Simply freeze your bags of seeds overnight. This will kill the moth larvae that are living in your finch food and eliminate the moth problem.

Chapter 3

Eating Well

Finches eat a tremendous variety of foods in the
wild and should have the same luxury in your
home. Some finches survive on a diet of seeds
and fresh water, but surviving isn't enough. If
you are going to keep finches as pets, you need to
be willing to take the time to feed them a varied
and nutritious diet. If you plan on breeding
finches, the nutritional requirements will be even
more diverse.

Although finches primarily eat seed, they need a varied diet for optimal health.

Proper Nutrition

Finches require all the same vitamins and minerals that other animals (including you) require to remain healthy. Many of these essential nutrients are not available in a strictly seed diet, and that means they need supplemental nutrition. Sprouted seeds, fruits, vegetables, insects, and supplements can be an important part of a finch's diet. If your birds are missing any of the essential vitamins, they can have extreme health problems. The good news is that all the important vitamins are easily available to add to finch diets in various ways.

Vitamin A is found in dark green and orange vegetables. Birds that have a deficiency of vitamin A develop respiratory and liver problems. These problems can be avoided by making the appropriate vegetables available to your birds. Generally, if their bodies need it, they will eat it.

Vitamin B is a complex of a dozen or so vitamins that include niacin as well as vitamins B_1 and B_2. Birds with a lack of B vitamins may produce fewer eggs and have poor feathering and growth. Dark green, leafy vegetables contain many of the vitamins necessary for good health and should be a daily offering to your birds.

Vitamin K is necessary to health, and a lack of it causes poor blood

Feed the Birds

Every day, you should supply your finches with:

• A variety of fresh seeds
• Dark green, leafy vegetables
• Chopped orange vegetables
• A variety of fresh fruit
• Fresh water
• Calcium
• Grit

Breeding birds also need live food. Keep mineral blocks available at all times.

clotting and anemia in birds. This vitamin is readily available in kale, broccoli, and other green vegetables.

These are just a few of the vitamins that are necessary to good health, but the trend is obvious. Essential vitamins are readily available in fresh leafy greens and other vegetables. So, although the possibility of sickness from a lack of proper nutrition is high, keeping your birds healthy by supplying a varied diet is a simple solution.

Finches also need carbohydrates and fats. Carbohydrates are the primary energy source, and therefore finches consume a great deal of them. This is one of the reasons that aviary finches tend to be healthy. Constant flying means the birds burn off the energy they consume instead of turning excess carbohydrates into fat. The same is true of eating food that has a great deal of fat, like many of the oil-based seeds. These are a great source of quick energy, especially in cooler weather, but birds in small cages indoors can quickly become obese.

Proteins are another crucial aspect of nutrition. There are certain proteins that the body cannot produce and which must be consumed in foods. Breeding and young birds require higher-than-normal levels of protein in their diets because of the stress of egg laying, rearing young, and growing.

Wild Diet

You have only to take a look at what finches eat in the wild to see that although seeds are an important component to their meals, variety is truly the spice of life. The part of the world the species came from also dictates their preferred diet. Some finches come from lushly vegetated areas with tremendous selection and plenty of insects. Others come from arid climates and harsh landscapes where their diet is much more limited. One thing is certain though: All finches eat more than three or four varieties of seeds in the wild.

In an average day, any species of finch will spend all day foraging. This means that whatever is available will be eaten, especially if it is particularly nutritious. Finches will nibble on the seed heads of grasses, pick at fruits and

FAMILY-FRIENDLY TIP
Let's Do It Together

Having your children help you feed the finches is a great way for them to learn about nutrition. Explain about all the different vitamins in the vegetables and why they are important to finches and humans as well. Explain how important variety is and why fresh water is important to all living things. Don't depend on your kids to feed the finches alone. Finches won't survive if they are forgotten. Make feeding the birds a family affair.

berries, find fallen grass seed on the ground, and also eat spiders, worms, and ants. This tremendous variety of food ensures that the birds consume all the vitamins, minerals, proteins, and carbohydrates that their busy little bodies require.

It is important that if you wish to breed a certain species of finch, or even just keep a healthy bird, you find out what they are likely to eat in the wild. Some finches feed their young on insects almost exclusively, so if you do not provide insects for them, they will not successfully rear young. Without the proper food, your finches may not even care to nest. Of course, zebra finches and society finches, along with a few other readily available species that have been domesticated, will live a seemingly normal life with nothing more than a good seed mix and water. But why force them to live a life with no choices when you know they could be feasting to their heart's content daily?

Pellets versus Seeds

Today, there are far more options than just seeds to feed the

birds. As we learn more and more about avian nutrition, scientists and nutritionists have worked to provide various food types that contain all the essential nutrients that our birds need. This is a difficult endeavor with so many different species of birds, however. One formulation may be great for zebra finches but be missing some of the important nutritional elements required by Gouldian finches. This has made feeding pelleted diets quite a controversy.

Pellet diets are produced for finches by several companies. The pellets have been manufactured to give finches all the necessary nutrients, but that doesn't mean that your finches will automatically eat them. These tiny bits of food do not look at all like seeds, and older finches will need to be converted to this diet if you wish to feed it to them. This can be dangerous

Here are three of the many components of a varied finch diet: pellets, millet, and egg food (clockwise from left).

Most finches—tri-colored munias are shown here—love millet spray. It's readily available at most pet stores.

and should be supervised by your veterinarian. It takes only 36 hours for smaller finches to starve to death, and most will starve rather than eat a food that they do not recognize or like.

Sometimes, soaking the pellets can make them more palatable to finches that are familiar with soft foods, encouraging them to try the pellets. Pellets soaked in water or orange juice may be more readily eaten. However, they will also spoil rapidly, especially in hot weather, so should not be left in the cage for more than a few hours. Some finch fanciers feel that switching to a pelleted diet is worth the extra effort because of the nutritional benefits, but everyone agrees that seeds should still be a supplement to a diet, along with fruits, vegetables, and insects.

Birdseed

There is a surprising variety of seeds available on the market, and all have different levels of fat and protein. Some are more palatable to different finches, and some are more nutritious than others. If you have only a few finches, you probably will want to buy premixed bags of finch seeds. It is important, if you buy premixed seeds, that you choose those that are specifically for finches. Some mixes for other birds will have seeds that are bigger or pointier and that will be ignored by your finches and scattered about. A finch mix will be primarily made up of several different millet seeds, with the addition of perhaps rape, Niger, oats, and other grains.

If you have a large number of finches, it is a good idea to create your

Millet Spray

Finches love millet spray. You can buy this spray at your favorite bird supply store or website. The seeds are still attached to the stalk and can be hung from the sides of indoor cages and from safe areas in aviaries. Finches may ignore their other treats, but they will never ignore millet spray.

own mix of seeds and perhaps even offer them individually so that the birds don't scatter them looking for their favorites. There are many different varieties of millet seeds, and all have a similar nutritional value. Use this to your advantage and determine which forms of millet appeal the most to your birds, and buy those millets individually. However, you will need more than millet in the mix, especially if your birds are breeding.

Seeds are divided up into cereal seeds—which are mainly grass seeds—and oil-based seeds. The cereal seeds are high in carbohydrates and lower in protein and fat. The oil-based

seeds contain more fat and very little carbohydrate. However, each of these ingredients is important. Therefore, a variety of seeds is critical.

Cereal Seeds

There are a number of cereal seeds that finches find appealing, with millet and canary seeds being the most common. Millet (as mentioned previously) is one of the main ingredients in a finch seed mix. They are a round seed that varies in color from whitish yellow to red. Another seed popular in finch mixes is canary seeds, which are oval shaped with pointy ends and are a bright yellow-brown color. These seeds are grown in Morocco (where they most frequently come from), Australia, Canada, and occasionally Britain.

Other cereal seeds can also be obtained and enjoyed by finches. Paddy rice, which is a flattish, broad, yellow-colored seed, is enjoyed by many finch species. The Java sparrows, also know as rice birds, enjoy these in particular. Groats, which are oats with the husk removed, are another supplement that larger finches enjoy.

Oil Seeds

Oil seeds are generally good for the plumage of birds, bringing out the gloss and shine of feathers. The most common oil seeds are sunflower seeds, but these are difficult for small finches to husk and eat. However, the hearts of sunflower seeds already husked are loved by all finches. Rape seed, Niger, and hemp are other oil seeds that are enjoyed by finches. Rape and Niger are frequently added to seed mixes during the breeding season.

The best way to decide what seeds to offer is to talk with your vet. Better yet, find a breeder with a great deal of success in breeding the species of finches that you are working with. Longtime finch breeders have most likely learned a great deal about nutrition and care over the years and will probably share their expertise and love of the little birds with you.

Choosing Seeds

With seeds coming from as far away as Morocco, it is a good idea to know how to determine if your seeds are fresh. Seeds that have gone bad or are going bad will either not be eaten, contain little nutritional value, or worse, make your birds ill. You'll want to look at the seeds before you buy them, if possible, and definitely check your seeds at home periodically.

Seeds that are fresh and of good quality should have a plump appearance and look polished. Withered and dried-out seeds should not be fed to your birds. Seeds that are especially dusty, dirty, or full of husks are not of good quality. They have likely not been cleaned properly. However, if you see webs in the seeds, this is not a cleaning issue but might be an infestation of moth larvae. This isn't dangerous, though; in fact, some finches might eat the worms. As long as the seeds seem fine and are not overly infested, the larvae can be killed by freezing. It pays to spend the money on high-quality seeds rather than saving a few dollars and giving your birds improper nutrition.

Oil seeds are good for your finch's plumage and bring out his natural shine. A shaft-tail finch is shown.

You can check the state of your seeds at home by sprouting them. Seeds that are dead and will not grow do not have much nutritional value. So if you are uncertain about your seeds, place a spoonful of them in the fold of a damp paper towel. Keep the towel moist and in a warm area for a couple of days. Most of these seeds should sprout. If they do not, then the seeds are dead and you should purchase fresh ones.

Check your seeds regularly and be sure to properly store them. Keep seeds in airtight containers in a cool, dry area. Improperly stored seeds can ultimately be deadly to finches. Rats can infest food and contaminate it with their droppings and urine. Old seeds that are allowed to become damp may encourage the growth of fungus and molds, which can be deadly to your birds.

Fruits and Vegetables

Whether you feed seeds, pellets, or a mixture of both, fruits and vegetables are a critical component to a healthy finch diet. Not all finches will eat all the different varieties of fruits and vegetables, but it doesn't hurt to offer them.

You will soon learn what your finches like to eat and what time of the year they tend to eat them. Finches may prefer only some foods during the breeding season, but make sure that you continue to offer a variety of foods all year.

Dark green and orange vegetables tend to be especially high in important vitamins, but there are many other possibilities. Spinach, greens, and other dark green, leafy vegetables can be offered. Finches may even bathe in wet leaves as well as nibble on them. Carrots, yams, peas, pumpkin, and cucumbers can be diced into small pieces for easy consumption. Fruits such as apple, melon, and grapes can also be offered. You can add almost any fruit or vegetable (except avocados, which are toxic to birds) to your finches diet for added variety and nutrition.

Greens

Growing greens for your finches is another excellent way to add

Finches will enjoy many leafy greens, including wild chickweed, dandelion, and grasses.

Don't Feed!

You need to give your finches a tremendous variety of foods, but there are some foods that you should avoid. If you decide to share some table food with your finches, take care. Stay away from sugar, salt, fatty human foods, chocolate, avocado, alcohol, and caffeinated beverages. These items are unhealthy for finches; avocados, chocolate, and alcohol are actually poisonous to them.

Preparing Fruits and Vegetables

Whatever fruits and vegetable you choose to feed your finches, make certain that they are free of pesticides. Finches are small birds with rapid metabolism, and the tiniest amounts of pesticides can harm them. Be sure to buy organic fruits and vegetables if you can, peel off the outer layer of greens like lettuce, and scrub hard-skinned vegetables. There are certain fruits that should never be fed unless they are organic, such as strawberries.

If you have neighbors that grow their own vegetables or have a local farmer's market, these can be two great sources of pesticide-free produce. Of course, nothing is more certain than growing your own. You can use frozen vegetables in a pinch, but they don't have as much nutrition as fresh ones. Avoid anything canned. Canned foods have even less nutrition and the dangerous addition of sodium. Fresh is always better.

It can be a good idea to arrange the fruits and vegetables separately in the bowl so that you can see what your finches are choosing to eat. If your finch is inside in a cage, you can clip greens, apples, and other chunks of fresh food to the side of the cage. In outside aviaries, however, it is better not to encourage finches to hang on the wire where predators might easily reach them.

nutrition and variety to their diet. This is the closest thing to the natural seeds finches eat in the wild that you can offer. Growing your own millet from seeds is relatively easy, and growing a potful would be greatly appreciated by your finches.

Some greens can also be collected. English rye grass, wild millets, chickweed, and dandelion are often appreciated. If you see wild birds eating from these seeds and grasses, chances are your birds will enjoy them as well. Just take care not to collect plants along roadsides or anywhere else that they may be contaminated by pesticides or the fumes from vehicles.

Sprouting seeds is easy and provides your finches with a nutritious snack.

Whatever vegetables you put in with your birds, be sure to remove them before they spoil. In the winter when it's cool, you can clean out the produce in the evening. In the summer, though, don't leave fresh fruits and vegetables in with your birds for more than a few hours. Spoiling food will attract pests and could make your birds sick.

Sprouted Seeds

Another great way to add nutrition to your birds' diet is to sprout seeds. Seeds that are germinated have a higher nutritional content than regular seeds and offer a nutrient-rich snack. There are many great seed sprouters on the market, and you can buy one to make your job simpler. However,

it isn't that difficult to make your own seed sprouter.

A mason jar with cheesecloth on the top works well for this. Fill the jar about one-quarter full with seed mix, and then fill the rest with water. Secure the cheesecloth over the opening with a rubber band. Leave the seeds to soak overnight.

In the morning, drain the water out through the cheesecloth, rinse the seeds, and then drain again. Do this a dozen times. Drain the jar and leave it on its side overnight. Repeat rinsing and draining the next day.

The seeds don't need to have growth showing to be nutritious, but you can continue to soak and rinse them for a few days for continued growth. Serve when short tails are showing. Be sure to sprout small batches to avoid spoilage, and store in the refrigerator. If the sprouts begin to smell rancid or look slimy, throw them away.

Eggs

Eggs are another great supplement for finches. Not only are they high in protein, but if you leave the shell as part of the package, they also have the added benefit of calcium. They can be fed periodically, and many different species of finches seem to enjoy them.

Boil eggs for a least half an hour before serving in order to kill any bacteria that might be in the egg. The boiled egg can be crushed—shell and all—and served. It can also be sliced or served whole. Some breeders note that their finches are more interested in the whites than the yolk.

Eggs should be only an occasional treat, however. There are other sources of protein that are more nutritious to birds. Some breeders also argue that chicken egg shells are not the safest form of calcium, because of the risk of salmonella. If you give your birds shells from raw eggs, you can get past this problem by microwaving or boiling the shell for a few minutes to kill any bacteria before you crush and serve.

Cooking for Your Birds

There are some forms of "people food" that can be beneficial to your finches. Bread soaked in milk, cheese, and whole wheat bread can be used to make mashes of seeds and any sort of medicine or supplement that your finches might need. They also contain protein.

If you want to make something fun for your finches to explore, a batch of "birdie bread" is a great treat. Buy a box of ready-mix corn bread and follow the directions. Leave the shell of the egg on, however, for the birds. You can add seeds and vegetables to the mix before you bake it. The bread that comes out of the oven is a regular birdie feast. The finches will have to pick through it to find their favorite treats, but this encourages their natural foraging behavior and keeps them occupied.

Live Food

Some finches absolutely need live food in order to rear their young. Others may make do without live food, but all your finches can benefit from the addition of insects and worms. Start with small batches to see what your birds prefer before you stock up.

All the forms of live food can make great additions to your finches' diet. You can also investigate fruit flies and ant pupae if you find a source for them. Waxbills that are rearing young will particularly appreciate live foods. Keep in mind that it is not safe to harvest whatever insects you can find in your home or yard. Those that you have bred or that have been bred commercially are safe and will be more likely to have a higher nutritional value based on what they have been fed.

Mealworms

Charcoal

Some finches—Gouldian finches especially—require charcoal granules. It is thought that they use it to detoxify their stomach and intestines. A small amount of charcoal can be placed in a dish and left out for the finches.

Eating Well

The orange-cheeked waxbill is one of the finches that requires live food for successful breeding.

Mealworms are one of the most common additions to finch diets. They are easy to get and even easy to breed yourself. However, they have a hard outer shell that is not digestible for many birds and especially young.

If you wish to supply your finches with mealworms regularly, you can raise them in a metal can filled with red bran and a slice of raw potato or apple. Change the potato or apple every day to prevent mold from growing. The worms are the larvae of a beetle and will breed under these conditions, producing eggs once some of the worms mature into adult beetles. Place them into a bowl and leave them out on a platform or on the floor of the aviary for the finches to eat.

Wax Worms and White Worms

Other worms may have more nutritional value for finches than mealworms do. Wax worms and white worms are a more suitable addition to the diet. They have softer skin and are easier to digest. Wax worms and white worms are not as readily available as mealworms. However, these days with the Internet, it is quite easy to search for suppliers of worms and insects in order to find the appropriate size for your finches. Feed these the same way you would the mealworms.

Crickets

Crickets are another insect that is frequently used as live food for finches. You can purchase crickets in a variety of sizes from hatchling on up to adult. You should be able to easily find the appropriate size for your flock of finches. Just be aware that adult crickets that elude the finches may set up shop and will find plenty to eat in your aviary. Buying younger crickets may help to avoid a cricket infestation.

You can dust crickets with vitamins to increase their nutritional value. To dust crickets, place some powdered supplement in a jar and add a few crickets. Gently shake the jar until the crickets are covered with the powder. They can also be placed in the refrigerator for a while to slow them down. Cold crickets will be easily caught up by your finches and can be fed in their indoor cage or out in the aviary in a bowl.

Vitamins and Minerals

A tremendous amount of care needs to be given to supplementing vitamins and minerals. If you have finicky finches that are not eating a variety of foods, they may need supplements. However, if they eat well and do not need supplementing, it can be dangerous. Overdoses of vitamins and minerals can be fatal.

There are two types of supplements: those that are added to drinking water and those that are added to food. Depending on the deficiency that you feel your flock may have, one may be better than the other. Both can be problematic in their own ways.

Powder-based supplements that are added to seeds may not stick well. They are best added to wetter food like greens and fruits. Still, birds may refuse the food. Liquid supplements added to water may have a strong taste and add color to the water, which some birds will refuse to drink. Also, if the water is exposed to sunlight, the vitamin may break down.

You should talk with your veterinarian before adding vitamin and mineral supplements to your finches' diet. If you do supplement, make sure to watch carefully that the birds are

Grit

There is some argument as to whether or not grit is a necessary component to finch diets. It is thought that they need it to grind down seeds in their gizzard. Some people think that grit may impact the crop and make finches sick that eat too much. However, most breeders still supply their finches with grit. Mineralized grit and oyster shell grit should both be supplied in a dish and changed every week, as finches tend to pick out the portions that they need and leave the rest.

Finches

drinking the medicated water or eating their medicated food. It would be easy to starve or dehydrate birds that refuse to eat or drink.

Mineral Blocks

Finches need certain minerals and trace elements to stay healthy. There is no reason to supplement their food with powdered minerals, however. The addition of an easily accessible mineral block in their cage will allow finches to pick at the block when necessary. Mineral blocks can be found in just about any pet store that has bird supplies.

Calcium

Breeding and growing finches need a constant supply of calcium. The best source of calcium for them is cuttlebone. Cuttlebone is not bone at all but is the internal shell of the cuttlefish, which frequently washes up on beaches.

Cuttlebone is rich in salt and calcium. It is also soft on one side and easily picked at and then swallowed by finches. It can be suspended with the soft side showing or crushed and put into a bowl. Cuttlebone can be found at almost any bird supplier, is inexpensive, and is easily consumed. There should always be a ready supply in finch enclosures, especially when birds are breeding.

Water

Of course, the other important component of proper nutrition is water. Finches should always have an ample supply of clean water for both bathing and drinking. Fresh water should be put out every morning, but don't be surprised when birds bathe in drinking water and drink their bathwater. The finches don't discriminate, so you'll have to make sure that all their water is consistently clean.

In the summer, change the water several times a day. Bathwater should not be deeper than 1 inch (2 to 3 cm), so that the finches feel comfortable bathing and will not drown. The bath pan should also be shallow and large so that they do not feel trapped when inside. However, this water will soil quickly, and in the summer, it will grow bacteria. Changing the water several times a day will keep disease from breaking out in your flock whether you have 2 birds or 20.

Summing UP

Your finches should always have ample

How Much Food?

Finches should always have enough food in their cages that there is some left over at the end of the day. Never ration finch food. It may be tempting when you see how much they waste, but it is not a good idea. Your finches cannot tell you what kind of seeds or which vegetables they need for getting the minerals and vitamins that their body has depleted. So make sure that there is always enough available for them to choose what they need.

Chapter 4

Looking Good

Healthy finches may not ever need help with grooming. They are well-groomed all on their own and happy to assist one another in the task. However, you should know exactly what a well-groomed finch looks like and be prepared to assist in grooming if necessary.

Feathers allow birds to fly and to regulate their body temperature. Here is a Java sparrow taking flight.

Feathers

Feathers are a critical component of a healthy finch. Feathers keep finches warm in cold weather and cool when the weather turns hot. Without feathers, finches cannot fly and therefore cannot get around in large areas, escape from dangerous situations, or breed. This means that feathers must always be kept in the best condition possible.

There are several different types of feathers. The fluffy feathers that are close to the body and keep the bird warm are called down feathers. The other feathers on the body are called contour feathers. These feathers are stiffer than down feathers, with a shaft running down the middle. Barbs shoot from the center of the shaft, and at the edges of these are barbules, which zip together and form

a solid but light surface. Even stiffer, sturdier feathers on the wings and tail allow the finches to fly.

This lightweight coat requires constant care. Feathers can be easily damaged by parasites, or other birds picking at them, and they wear down with use and exposure to the elements. So birds have to keep them in great shape as well as preen them—zipping them back together so that they are optimal for warmth and flying.

Bathing

Bathing is an important behavior in finches and an important aspect of feather care as well. Most healthy finches will bathe occasionally, and some species of finches will bathe three or more times a day if the mood strikes them.

Bathing involves lifting feathers away from the body and either splashing in water or enjoying a shower. Drenched feathers become cleaner. Bathing carries debris like dirt, feather dust, and skin particles off the feathers. Bathing also assists in controlling lice. Bathing can be important to birds that are incubating or brooding. By getting their underfeathers wet, the finches can control the humidity in the nest, which is an important factor in hatching eggs and keeping the chicks healthy.

Bathing finches will lift their tail and dip their hind end into the water

repeatedly. They will then dip their head into the water and splash it onto their back. Soon they will start flapping their wings and getting water droplets everywhere. There is no doubt when watching finches bathe that they are in a state of complete bliss. They will continue with this behavior until they are almost too wet to fly, then will find a sunny branch to dry out on and preen.

Bath Pans

Bath pans are the easiest way to get finches bathing. If you have a single pair of finches kept inside your home, there are a variety of birdbaths to choose from. Try several until you find one that your bird enjoys. There are birdbaths that hook to the outside of the cage and are set up for the finches to enter, but all the water splashing will remain outside the cage, keeping food dry. There are bowls that can be set on the floor of the cage as well, and some even have mirrors to entice the birds in. Of course, any shallow dish that you can find in the kitchen and that will fit in the cage might work, as well.

If you have an aviary full of finches, a large shallow bath pan will work well. Even one of those concrete birdbaths meant for gardens will work nicely if it fits in your aviary. The trick is that the bigger the bath pan, the better. Once one finch gets in, chances are everyone else will want to join the pool party. Once a finch starts bathing, none of the other birds can seem to resist, so the more birds that can fit in the bath, the more will be bathing.

Don't Clip!

It may seem tempting to clip your finches' wings. You may think they would be easier to catch and to tame. However, finches cannot climb on the bars of their cage like a parrot. They have no way to get around without their wings. They need them to hop around from perch to perch and to feel secure. Finches that are clipped will be clumsy and stressed. Don't clip your finches' wings!

Some bird baths attach to the outside of the cage and help prevent your finches from soaking their cage and food.

the water. Don't give up if the finches don't take to it right away. Try again from time to time, and chances are the finches will decide that a bath isn't a bad idea. Finches that enjoy being misted will look just like a finch in a bath pan. They will shake their tail and wings trying to get water on every last bit of themselves.

If your birds refuse to bathe, they may not like your water. Some tap waters have quite a bit of chlorine in them. If the birds are outside, just leave the water out for a while. The chlorine will slowly dissipate into the air. Inside, you can try using bottled water or running the water through a purifier.

Misting

If you cannot get your indoor birds to get into a birdbath or even bathe in their water, it is a good idea to teach them to enjoy a misting. Birds that do not bathe are generally in less-than-satisfactory feather condition. They may look messy and unkempt. Their feathers and skin may become dry and uncomfortable.

A plant mister works well for spraying finches. Move all the food out of the cage so that it doesn't get wet, and try giving the birds a little spritz. The finer the mist, the more likely the finches will take to it. Be careful, however. If your finches fly around the cage frantically, they are not enjoying their bath—you are just stressing them out.

Lightly mist a corner of the cage away from the finches and see if, after a while, they wander over and test

FAMILY-FRIENDLY TIP

Lets Do It Together

Grooming is not a kid's job. Finches are delicate and tiny. Grooming is a precision task that involves careful handling of the bird. Children can hand you tools and be on hand if they are interested and want to help, but they should not be allowed to catch the finch or clip the nails and beak.

Finches enjoy sunbathing, and sunlight is good for their feathers, skin, and bones.

Dust Baths

If your finches are outdoors, you may see them enjoying a dust bath. This probably seems like a good way to counteract a good dousing with water, but it is quite the contrary. Dry, fine sand or fine earth seems to be appealing to them. The birds roll in the fine dirt just as they would in water, covering the feathers with the fine silt and then shaking it out. Some experts think that this behavior might help control feather lice and keep feathers in excellent shape. Some species even bathe first in dust and then in water. You may have even seen common house sparrows in a patch of fine sand enjoying a dusting. Your finches may enjoy the same.

Ant Baths

An incredibly interesting behavior you may or may not witness outdoor finches partaking in is an ant bath. This has been well documented in many birds, including species of finches, like the waxbills. The bird will stand on an anthill or possibly grab an insect from a line of ants, crush it, and rub the ant through their feathers. This is always done with nonbiting varieties of ants. Once the finch is finished with the ant, it will either eat it or drop it. No one knows exactly why birds do this, but it is speculated that the acid in the ants may kill parasites. Or there may be some other secretion from the ants that aids in feather maintenance.

Sunbathing

Although finches seem to be perpetually busy throughout the day, sunbathing is important, not only to grooming but to finches' overall health. If your finches can find a patch of sun, whether they are in an aviary or inside your home, they are likely to spend some time with their feathers spread, soaking up the sun.

Sunbathing is a great way to dry feathers after bathing or even to bake parasites off the feathers. More important, finches and all birds need sunlight to create vitamin D. This vitamin is a crucial factor in being able to absorb calcium, which is why we drink milk that is fortified with vitamin D. Birds need to spend time in sunlight, but light through a glass window is not sufficient. Some of the sunlight's vitality is lost when it comes through the glass. So it is important that you either allow your birds time in the sun or provide them with a full-spectrum light for a little bit of sunbathing.

Preening

Preening is another important aspect of grooming feathers. Finches have an oil gland at the base of their tail that produces oils specifically designed for feather care. You will see a healthy finch taking time to rub their beak on the gland and then spread the oil on some feathers. They will repeat this behavior often, until every feather that covers their body has been oiled and groomed. This oil keeps the feathers supple and perhaps even waterproofs them.

The Expert Knows

Molting

Imagine if you grew a whole new head of long hair every year or even twice a year! Sure, we shed, but it isn't like molting. In the short span of a few weeks, finches change over all their feathers from old to new. This is molting. No wonder it's a stressful time. Make sure finches have plenty of good food and a warm stress-free environment during this difficult time.

Preening is a behavior that pairs of birds will indulge in. When new feathers are growing out, they begin as pin feathers, which are the feathers rolled up in a sheath as they grow. These sheaths, similar to the tip of a shoelace, must be cracked off for the feathers to unfurl. Mostly, birds can take care of this preening necessity themselves, with the exception of their head feathers. With all those uncomfortable pin feathers, it's great to have a buddy to take care of the ones you cannot reach. Not only is this important for feather care, but it is also a way in which pairs bond.

Plucking

When you have several birds together, watch out for plucking. Preening is a natural and important behavior, but a bird that has patches of missing feathers is probably being plucked. This can be a sign of aggression between finches. This sort of aggression can escalate, and the aggressors should be removed. The exception is when hens pluck their own belly to create a brood patch. This behavior is normal. Keep in mind that with other plucking, there is also the possibility that the plucked bird is ill and the other birds are picking on it. You may want to remove the plucked bird and evaluate its health.

Molting

Looking good and feeling healthy involves changing feathers every year. Most finches will completely change their feathers once, and sometimes twice, a year. Feathers grow from follicles in the skin, just like human hair does. A feather falls out and a new one grows in behind it. This is called molting. This allows worn feathers to be replaced with brand new ones.

Only healthy birds will molt, because growing new feathers takes a great deal of energy. Finches tend to begin molting after the breeding season for this reason as well. The body is no longer under the demands of laying eggs and feeding young. Instead, all extra energy can be focused on growing new feathers. The feathers are not dropped all at once.

This Lady Gouldian finch is in the process of molting. Notice the pin feathers emerging on her head.

It generally takes a month or more to replace them, as they are dropped out in small amounts, but during this time period, finches may be under more stress, become more easily chilled, and require higher levels of protein and other nutrients.

Finches that are molting should mostly look normal. You may notice the birds looking a little scruffy, but they should not have bald patches. Bald patches are a sign of sickness or that another bird is plucking them. Any spot with missing feathers should have pin feathers coming in and not be entirely bare. Young birds in their first molt may look a little more disheveled, because they are molting as well as still growing, and that is a lot of strain to put on the body. The best thing you can do for molting birds is to make sure that they have excellent nutrition.

Less Stress, Better Health

Mostly, your birds will take care of grooming themselves as long as you provide appropriate nutrition and ample water. However, there may be times when you need to trim nails and beaks. Remember, though, that finches are easily stressed.

Birds that are overly stressed are more likely to become ill. Finches that are used to people are more likely to tolerate grooming without as much stress, but catching them can still be a stressful event. It is better to avoid grooming your birds if you can. If it is the nails and beak that need to be tended to, however, you should take extreme care in catching your bird.

Catching Your Finches

There are several ways to catch your finches, but not all of them are recommended. Many people use this first method, which is to chase finches until they are worn out and easy to catch. Obviously, this method is highly stressful and not recommended. If your finch is in a smaller cage, try to reach in and corner the finch, catching it quickly before it is too stressed.

If you have finches in a larger aviary, netting is another option. However, if you are not good at using a net, you could stress out your entire flock. If netting is your only option, but sure to remove perches and other obstacles that might get in the way of the swinging net. Try to corner the bird that needs to be netted, while keeping the net close to your side, and then catch the finch quickly, but move the net slowly. If the finch comes to an abrupt stop inside the net, it could be injured.

A better method of catching birds is to use the darkness. If your finches are in a small cage, take them into a windowless room and turn off the lights. Make sure you know where the finch is in the cage when it gets dark, and grab the bird quickly before it moves and with care so that you do not injure it. Catching aviary birds in the dark can also work if you have a friend with a flashlight, but take care. If you startle all the birds, they may continue to thrash in the dark and injure themselves.

If you grab finches for grooming, try to do it early in the morning or late in the evening when it is cool. This way, finches will not overheat. If you use a net, make sure that the rim is soft and padded. A deep net is a good idea, as finches can quickly slip back out.

Handling Finches

Handling finches can be tricky and may take some practice. Finches need to be held firmly so that they do not escape, but with a great deal of care so that the bird is not injured. Try to hold the finch so that her head protrudes between your thumb and forefinger, while the rest of your hand wraps around her body. Don't hold the finch too loosely or she will easily escape your grasp.

Trimming Nails

Once you have the finch firmly in your grasp, you can trim her nails, if needed. Some finches that live in reeds in their natural habitat have nails that grow quickly and spiral as they grow out. This sort of growth is helpful to birds that grasp upright slippery reeds but is not necessarily helpful in an aviary. Overgrown toenails can get caught in the wires of the aviary or the cage. Birds may injure toes or feet, or even hang upside down and die. Trimming overgrown nails is very important.

With the finch in your hand, gently pull her foot free and hold between your finger and thumb. Separate the

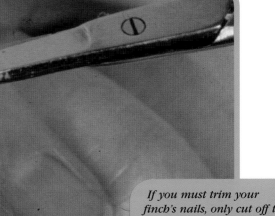

If you must trim your finch's nails, only cut off the tips and be careful to avoid the quick.

toes and locate where the blood ends in the toenail. You can tell this by holding the toes up to the light. The nail is see-through up to the quick, where the blood starts. You do not want to clip below this quick or the finch will bleed. The clear part of the nail is dead and can be safely trimmed.

Using a pair of human toenail clippers or a guillotine-style trimmer will work well. Scissors are best avoided for trimming nails. Carefully clip the nail above the quick. Keep some styptic powder or cornstarch

Fragile Finches

It may sound like finches are incredibly fragile, but the truth is that if they are well taken care of, they can be hardy birds. If your finches have a warm, dry, clean environment and plenty of fresh food, they will thrive. If you give them the closest thing you can to their natural environment in the wild, you will see that finches are not fragile at all. With the proper care, they are robust little creatures.

handy. If you do nip past the quick, dip the nail in either powder and it will quickly stop the bleeding.

If you continue to have difficulty with overgrown toenails in your finches, consider changing perches. Rough wooden perches with varying width or concrete perches can help with wearing down the nails naturally.

Trimming the Beak

Keep a careful eye on the shape of your finches' beaks. Overgrown beaks can make it difficult for finches to eat and will ultimately kill them if their beaks are not reshaped. An overgrown beak will usually have one mandible longer than the other, or the bill will look crossed.

Using a pair of scissors or nail clippers, cut the longer mandible to fit the shorter one, or if the bill is crossed, trim it back to its original shape. A file can be used to touch up the bill and get the upper and lower mandible to match. Take care not to cut too much off the beak or you may injure the underlying bone. Finches are so small that this can be tricky and possibly dangerous. So if you don't have experience, it is a good idea to take your bird to the vet.

If you continue to have issues with overgrown bills with your finches, you probably need to change the perches. Finches whittle down their beaks by rubbing them on rough surfaces. Placing natural or concrete perches in the cage or aviary may encourage birds to keep their bills in good order.

Grooming Health Check

If you must clip your finches' nails and beak, take the time to do a health check. Thoroughly examine your bird's body for any lumps, bumps, lesions, abrasions, or discharge. Check to make sure your finch doesn't feel too thin or too plump.

Health Check

When you have caught a finch, it's a good idea to inspect her thoroughly for any signs of illness or trouble. Check wings, feet, legs, abdomen, vent, breast, and head for any signs of swelling or other problems. Investigate feathers for signs of lice or mites. Check to see that the breast is well-fleshed and that the bird seems to be properly nourished. This is a good opportunity to see if your finches are healthy.

If you have only a few finches and feel uncomfortable about catching them to trim toenails or beaks, this is also an excellent opportunity to take your birds to the vet. An avian veterinarian can groom your birds for you and also do a well-check. Take advantage of this chance to get to know your veterinarian and let him or her get to know you before you have a health problem to bring to the vet's office.

Chapter 5

Feeling Good

Finches are often considered fragile birds. The truth is that given the proper diet and environment, they are quite hardy. It is unusual to have a sick bird if your flock or pair is given the proper care. However, it is important to know how to recognize the signs of a sick finch and know where to get help for your bird immediately. A bird that looks ill should always be considered an emergency.

What Makes Finches Sick

If you care for your finches properly, chances are that if you purchased healthy birds, they will remain healthy birds. Several things encourage disease to establish itself into your finches' environment. By taking simple precautions, you avoid many forms of finch illness. Prevention is always the easiest medicine.

Too Many Birds

Overcrowding is a prime reason for finches becoming sick. Environments with too many birds get dirty faster and are hard to keep clean. Food and water dishes are quickly contaminated with feces and food, creating a bacterial soup that could make all your birds ill.

When many birds are housed together, it is easier to spread disease quickly. The birds are in close quarters and are forced to be in contact with one another. In normal conditions, a sick finch will isolate itself from the others, choosing a quiet, undisturbed place to perch. When a cage is overcrowded, all the other finches are likely to come close enough to be infected.

Overcrowding is stressful on the finches. They may pick on one another and constantly flit about as they jockey for a position on a good perch. Stressed finches have an impaired immune system and are more likely to get ill. If you choose to breed your finches, do not let their

environment become overcrowded as more birds are added to the mix.

Contaminated Food

Spoiled food is another reason finches get ill. Scrimping on the cost of food could cost you your birds. Don't spend less on overripe fruit or cheap birdseed. Food that is rotten or stale could collect bacteria, fungus, and other pathogens that might kill your birds.

Buying excellent food but not taking care to store it properly could also lead to contaminated food. Make sure your food is kept fresh,

Overcrowding is one of the major reasons finches become ill.

and always check that it is in good condition before you dole it out to your birds. Once it is in the cage, it should be cleaned out before it starts to spoil as well.

Cleanliness

In the end, the most important thing you can do to keep your finches healthy is to keep their environment clean. Clean fresh water and food will not contain any diseases that can kill your birds. If you are sure to clean up food that has been scattered on the

Teflon Dangers

Watch out for anything in your house that has a Teflon coating. In fact, throw Teflon pots and pans away. When overheated, Teflon emits a gas that is instantly deadly to birds—finches with their tiny respiratory system, especially. It takes forgetting a pan on the stove only once to kill your finches. Space heaters, irons, and other products contain Teflon, and bird owners should avoid these products or take great care with them.

floor of the cage or aviary, you will avoid illness. You may know better than to eat food that isn't in a bowl or on a plate, but finches are happy to find things to eat on the ground.

How to Know When Your Finch is Sick

Sometimes, though, in spite of your best efforts, you may find yourself with an ill bird. The sooner you can recognize sickness in your birds, the quicker you can get your bird help. Learn the signs of illness.

When you first get your finches, be sure to spend many hours observing them. You will quickly learn what happy, healthy finches look like and which daily activities they prefer. Watching your finches and understanding what their normal behavior is will help you quickly determine when your finch isn't looking quite right.

The sooner you discover that a finch is ill, the better your chances of saving her. Finches naturally hide symptoms of illness and are good at this. Finches that look ill are the first to draw attention to themselves and be snatched from the flock by predators. Looking healthy for as long as possible is a great defense in the wild, but in your home, it means that by the time your finch looks ill, she is truly sick and needs immediate attention. If you can spot an ill finch quickly, you may be able to get her the medication she needs before it is too late.

Behavioral Changes

A finch that is sick may exhibit some behavioral changes that indicate she is not feeling well. Finches that seem less active may be ill. Take note if your finch is not moving about. Finches that are completely inactive are definitely ill. If your finch is fluffed up in a corner and not moving, especially if she doesn't respond to your presence, you should immediately get her medical attention.

Any other behavioral changes should be noted as well. Some may be obvious. Birds that have stopped eating or have begun to drink water excessively may have a problem. If your bird is unable to stand, staying at the bottom of the cage, or has drooping wings or convulsions, she needs immediate attention. More subtle behavior changes should be noted, for example, if your bird becomes unusually quiet and is no longer making noises, or if your male finch has stopped singing.

Physical Changes

Watch for physical changes in your finch as well. You should examine your bird from outside the cage daily. Look at her eyes, nares, and vent especially. Feather loss, or swelling and discharge around the eye, is an indication of sickness. The same is true of the nares. If your bird's nostrils are swollen or have any sort of crusty or wet discharge, the finch has a problem. Debris or feces caked around the vent area are an indication of sickness. Any enlargement or swelling of the body can indicate a problem as well.

Finches have delicate feet and legs, so be sure to check how your bird lands and stands on the perch. If she is favoring one leg, it could be injured. The same is true if she shifts on her feet. Watch for swelling, abrasions, and lesions on her toes and feet.

How to Examine Finch Droppings

Your first means of determining illness is by looking at the droppings of your finch. There will often be changes in the urine, urates, and feces of your bird's droppings. If you are familiar with what your finch's droppings look like normally, you will easily be able to notice changes. Changes in droppings frequently indicate illness.

A finch that keeps her feathers fluffed up all the time is likely ill.

When keeping finches in a group, watch out for any aggression. Fighting between finches can cause serious foot injuries.

First you need to be able to recognize the three parts of your bird's droppings. Feces are food waste material from the digestive tract. This is the only solid part of the dropping and is normally tubular shaped, although this can vary some. The color of the feces depends on whether the bird is on a seed diet or a pelleted diet. Birds that eat seeds will have dark green or black feces, and those that eat pellets will have feces that are softer and brownish.

The liquid part of the droppings are made up of urine and urates. The urates are a creamy white color and fairly thick in consistency. The urine is clear and liquid, like water. Sometimes, the urine and urates will mix, and other times, the urine will surround the

First Aid

It is a good idea to keep a stocked first-aid kit for emergencies. Make sure you have these things on hand:

- Antibiotic ointment
- Alcohol
- Bandages and gauze
- Cotton balls
- Cotton swabs
- Hydrogen peroxide
- Styptic powder
- Tweezers

urates. You should get in the habit of examining your bird's droppings.

Although the consistency and color of the three parts varies some, depending on what the bird is eating and whether or not she is stressed, you will be able to recognize when there is a serious difference in how her droppings look. If the color of her droppings match the color of her food, don't be alarmed; it is most likely normal. Just keep an eye on her.

There are some obvious signs of sickness, however. If the urates or urine are green or yellow, your bird may have a liver disease. Red indicates internal bleeding or kidney disease. Watch for feces that are pea green, white, or gray, which could indicate internal disease. If there is undigested food in the feces, this is an indication of an infection in the digestive tract. Watch for diarrhea where the feces is formless or all three

Feeling Good

parts are mixed together. Keep in mind as well that fresh feces should not smell bad. If they do, your bird probably has a bacterial infection. Be sure to take samples of these irregular droppings with you to the vet. You can use a tongue depressor and put them in a plastic bag to keep them from drying out, but try to keep them intact.

Emergency First Aid

If you have a bird that is obviously ill, and you cannot get to the vet immediately, there are a few things you can do to make her comfortable and help her feel better. However, if there is any way at all to get her to the vet, take her. If you decide to wait until tomorrow to see if she gets better, there is a good chance that she will die.

The two most important considerations for temporary care before you can get your finch to your veterinarian are heat and food. You need to get your bird into a warm place and make sure that she is eating and drinking.

Finches utilize a great deal of energy to keep warm, and a sick bird may not have the energy to spare. Get her into a hospital cage, a small cage with a heat source, right away. You can set the cage half on and half off of a heating pad, giving her the option of moving in and out

of the warmer area of the cage. You can also use an infrared light bulb. The cage should be kept at 86° to 91°F (30° to 33°C). If the finch is too warm, she will hold her wings away from her body and pant. If this happens, move the heat source further away and try to cool the cage a few degrees.

The other thing your finch needs is food and water. If she has been sick for a few days and not showing signs, she may not have been eating and drinking. Make sure that there is water easily available, and scatter food on the floor of the hospital cage. You may even try hand-feeding her some of her favorite food. Remember that it takes only a few days for a finch to starve to death!

Getting Your Finch to the Vet

It is best to have a small transportation cage on hand all the time. Many suppliers make small cages that are

Finches

Once a finch, such as this fluffed-up violet-eared waxbill, shows any signs of illness, it is already very sick and needs medical attention.

specifically for transporting small birds like finches to shows as well as to the vet. You can also use one of those old-fashioned cardboard boxes that some breeders and pet stores use to send finches home with you. Whatever you choose, make sure that it will be easy to get your finch in and out of without losing her.

Make sure that she stays warm on the way to the vet. If she is in a cage, cover the cage with a towel so that there are no drafts. It is important to keep stress at a minimum, so carry the box or cage carefully; do shake or bounce it. Keep it covered so that she won't be startled by any new sights.

Avian Veterinarians

Hopefully, you've done your homework and already found an avian veterinarian. There is no worse time to be looking for a good vet than when your bird is ill. You should already have a relationship with a vet who is familiar with the breed of finches you have and with whom you have already developed a rapport.

Finding an Avian Vet

It isn't enough to take your bird to a vet who works only with dogs and cats. Avian medicine is specialized and is constantly evolving. You need a veterinarian who is familiar with all the current advancements in avian medicine, the tests that can be given, and the treatments. There is so much involved with understanding avian medicine that it isn't really fair to expect a dog and cat veterinarian

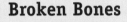

Broken Bones

If your finch breaks a bone, you may be limited in your options for what to do. Most veterinarians are unlikely to agree to operate or set the bone. Finches have a good chance of not surviving surgery or anesthesia because of their small size and delicate body. The best thing to do is avoid broken bones. Finches most commonly break bones by flying into walls and windows after escaping or because of calcium deficiency.

without a bird specialty to be familiar with all the aspects of treating your birds. Just think, your doctor has to know only about humans. Your vet has to understand a variety of different animals and their illnesses.

Finding an avian vet can be a little tricky, but you should do it before you get finches. If you buy a finch, especially if it is an expensive exotic such as a Gouldian finch, you will most likely have a health guarantee and need to get the bird into a vet within three days. If something is

FAMILY-FRIENDLY TIP

Emergency!

It can be scary for children when finches are sick. Explain the situation and immediately get the sick finch into a hospital cage if you cannot get her to the vet right away. Keep the finch confined so that if she is injured, she cannot injure herself further, and if she has an infection, your other finches will not be infected. Make sure she has food and water and keep her warm. Be positive and honest about the situation, and let your child be involved by helping to bring food and water. If your child accompanies you and the beloved finch to the vet, clearly explain to him or her ahead of time what may happen during the visit. This will help reduce your child's anxiety at this stressful time.

wrong with the finch, you'll get your money back. And even more important, you'll know not to put the bird in with your other finches. So talk with other local finch breeders, or join a bird club and ask which avian vet everyone uses. You're sure to get some good advice. If you don't have this sort of local resource, you can check with the Association of Avian Veterinarians at www.aav.org and find the appropriate vet closest to you.

Information for Your Vet

When you are on your way to the vet with your sick finch, make sure you take all the information you can. Time is of the essence, and the more information you have to give your veterinarian, the easier time he or she will have diagnosing the disease, ordering tests, and suggesting medication. If you have a flock of finches, this is especially important. Your entire flock could be at risk.

Write down any behavior changes, food you have been feeding, and your finch's current activity. Was your finch about to lay an egg, brooding, or rearing young? Is it a young unmated bird? Note any problems that you've had with other finches if you keep a flock. What signs of illness have you noticed? If possible, bring a stool sample. All of this will help your vet. Once the finch is in the vet's office, she will be out of a comfortable environment and some of the symptoms may no longer be obvious.

What to Expect at the Vet

It is really important that you take your bird to the vet rather than call with symptoms and ask for a diagnosis. The vet will most likely not be able to tell you what is wrong over the phone. Even if she can, you may not be seeing the most obvious illness. It is likely that a sick finch has more than one problem. Your vet can test for everything in her office and give your bird the best care possible.

The veterinarian will likely weigh the finch and check her breast bone to see how thin she is. The vet may take cultures from the mouth and vent or anywhere else that has discharge. The tests will help your vet determine what is making your finch ill. Don't be shy about asking what tests are being done and gleaning any information you can from your vet. These answers may help you determine better ways to notice if your finch is sick in the future.

What to do if Your Finch Dies

Sometimes, despite our best care and efforts, we have the terrible experience of losing a finch. Finches have relatively short lives compared with some birds—only 6 to 8 years—although they do on occasion live much longer. If you have an older finch, it may have died of natural causes associated with old age. If there is any question and you have other finches, it is a good idea to take the finch in for a necropsy, just in case. A necropsy will allow your avian vet to analyze what killed the finch and suggest if it might be contagious or perhaps if there is something in the environment that should be changed for the rest of your finches.

Common Finch Ailments

Unfortunately, there are a variety of illnesses and conditions that can afflict finches. Here are a few of the more common ones.

Parasites

Parasites are animals that feed off the blood or other nutrients in their host animal's body. A small infestation of parasites is often not a problem, but as the infestation becomes larger, the parasites can use so much of the host's nutrients that the host becomes ill or dies. Generally, parasites are simple to treat as long as they are discovered and treated early.

Feather Mites and Lice

Lice and mites are a common problem in finches, but for the most part, they are not dangerous, just uncomfortable. Some lice are species specific, and others can be found on most any bird. Sometimes, they can be seen as tiny specks moving through feathers, but some types of lice cannot be

77

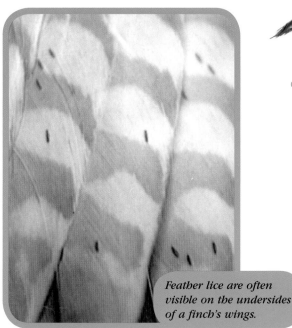

Feather lice are often visible on the undersides of a finch's wings.

seen by the naked eye and require a microscope to see. Lice can be irritating to birds, causing them to preen excessively or frequently shake their feathers.

Mites, specifically red mites, can be more problematic for finches. These tiny arachnids feed on blood and are easily seen with the naked eye. They are nocturnal, however, so you must check your birds after dark. The mites will appear as pepper flake–sized red or brown specks moving about on the bird's feathers. Mites, just like lice, irritate birds, making them restless. A serious infestation, however, can cause anemia and weakness in birds.

Feather and body lice and mites can be taken care of easily. You can find a safe spray for your birds and their cage or aviary at most any pet store or bird supplier. Just spray the bird and the infected area, and the mites and lice will be killed. These pests are easily spread from one bird to another, so make sure, if you have multiple birds, that every finch gets treated.

Air Sac Mites

Air sac mites are a respiratory problem that can occur in most finches but are especially common in Gouldian finches and canaries. These pesky mites set up shop in the air sacs, trachea, and sometimes even the lungs of finches. The parasites clog the airways and make it difficult to breathe. An infected finch will tire quickly and may be seen gasping for air.

The mites are spread only through oral exchange between birds. So parents feeding chicks, and pairs engaged in courtship behavior, may share the infection. It may even be spread through drinking water. If the infection of mites is not treated, the finch will ultimately die. Air sac mites are usually treated with ivermectin, but you should consult your veterinarian.

Scaly Face and Beak

Scaly face and beak is an infestation of mites that is more common in parakeets, but finches can also be infected. There are several different species of mites that cause this condition in birds, but it's a mite with the scientific name *Knemidocoptes jamaiscensis* that is specifically a problem to finches. The mites lay eggs in the skin of the finches' face, and when the mites hatch, they cause swelling, lesions, and a crusty coating to the skin. Finches with heavy infestations can have permanently damaged skin and may even die. Like feather and body mites, these mites can

A Replacement Finch

If you have a pair of finches in your home and one dies, you may be wondering what to do. It is not true that birds will pine away and die if they lose their mate. It is also not true that they will not accept a younger or older finch as a new partner. So, it is your decision. If you wish to have a pair again, introduce another finch, but your remaining bird will likely be fine without a new mate.

Finches kept outdoors have a higher chance of contracting parasites than those kept indoors.

also be treated with sprays purchased in pet stores and through bird suppliers.

Worms

There is a tremendous variety of parasitic worms that can infest your finch, and all can be deadly if not treated. They include tapeworm, round worm, thread worm, and gape worm. The most common of these is the tapeworm. Worms are often easily diagnosed by spotting worm segments in feces or in your finches' mouths.

Worm infestations are transmitted by eating infested insects. This is one of the reasons that you should not collect your own live food for your finches. Most live food suppliers keep their insects worm-free. However, if your finches are in an outdoor aviary, they can still eat an occasional bug and get an infestation of worms. If this goes untreated, the worms will eventually absorb more nutrients than your finch can eat, killing her. It is a good idea to treat finches for worms on occasion as a preventative measure, especially if you have an outdoor flock. Your vet can suggest or prescribe an appropriate medication.

Coccidiosis

Coccidiosis is the name for a variety of protozoan parasites that set up shop in the intestines of finches. They ultimately cause massive swelling and bleeding of the gut. Finches that have coccidiosis will exhibit listlessness, lethargy, weight loss, diarrhea, and dehydration. Their droppings even may be bloody. Ultimately, infected birds may die. Birds that are infected may not show symptoms until they

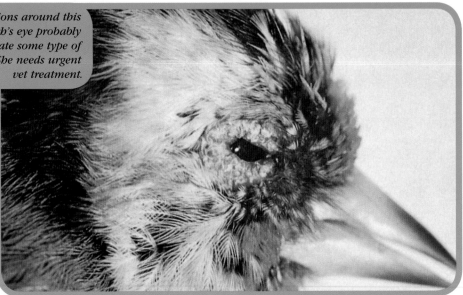

are under stress, so coccidiosis is often problematic in a breeding flock.

A vet can diagnose coccidiosis, and it is easily treated, but it is prevalent in the environment. Indoor birds are less likely to contract the illness, but aviary birds can easily be infected by wild birds if their droppings get into the aviary. This is a good reason to have birds well checked by an avian veterinarian periodically.

Fungal Infections

There are many natural agents in the environment that are in your aviary and your finch's body. Most of these are harmless, but some can cause infection in a compromised finch. If a finch is already ill or weakened from breeding or other stress, sometimes natural fungi can cause dangerous infections.

Aspergillosis

Aspergillus is a common fungus in most environments but flourishes in damp, unventilated areas. A finch that contracts aspergillosis—infection with *Aspergillus*—will have fungus growth throughout their respiratory system. Finches with this infection will have difficulty breathing and will tire quickly. You will need your avian veterinarian to diagnose this disease, which will most likely be deadly. It is difficult to treat, and if you have a flock of birds and an individual has a case of aspergillosis, you should create a drier, cleaner environment before more birds are infected.

Candidiasis

Yeast (*Candida*) is a common fungus in the environment that can be a source of mouth, digestive tract, and respiratory infection. Just like aspergillosis, candidiasis (or thrush) is an infection that usually occurs because of another underlying problem. If your bird is stressed, undernourished, or sick with another disease, the yeast that naturally occurs in her body may begin to multiply unchecked and cause problems. The infection will cause the bird to become listless and look ill. Frequently, thrush is also caused by the use of antibiotics, which kill the bacteria that normally keep natural yeast in the body in check.

Stress

Many of the illnesses that are common in finches are also common in the environment. This means that at any time, finches can succumb to a parasitic, fungal, or bacterial infection. Most finches stay healthy unless their immune system is compromised. Stress is the most common starter of illness because it weakens the immune system. Try to avoid situations that might cause stress to your finches.

Avian Gastric Yeast (Megabacteria)

Once called megabacteria because it didn't respond to antibiotics and was thought to be a large bacterium, vets now understand that this elusive problem in finches and other birds is actually a fungal infection, specifically a yeast infection. This disease causes birds to become lethargic, "go light" and lose weight, have difficulty eating, and eventually die. Your veterinarian can diagnose this disease and prescribe the best medication to treat it. However, just like candidiasis, it is often a secondary infection, so make sure that you are treating any other sicknesses.

Bacterial Infections

Bacteria, just like fungi, are naturally occurring organisms in the environment. In a reasonably clean environment with a good supply of food and fresh water, most finches have a healthy enough immune system to battle harmful bacteria. Sometimes, though, a particularly virulent bacterium is introduced to the environment, or a finch's immune system is compromised, and a bacterial infection gets out of control.

A finch with a bacterial infection will often have yellow or bright green diarrhea as well as discharge from its eyes or mouth. If you suspect a bacterial infection in your bird, then you should take her to the vet. Your vet will be able to do a culture and determine what the bacterium is and what antibiotic will work best to cure

Feeling Good

Finches

it. Consider all bacterial infections contagious and isolate your finch from others until it is finished being treated with antibiotics.

Egg Binding

If you are breeding your finches (and even if you are not), you should be aware of the possibility of egg binding in hens. Egg binding is when a hen cannot pass an egg that she is carrying. Hen finches may lay eggs even if there is no male present, so it is important that you are aware of this potential and deadly problem.

A hen that is egg bound will look lethargic and fluffed up, and her tail may bob or raise repeatedly as she tries to pass the egg. Egg binding is most commonly caused by an improper diet, more specifically a diet lacking calcium, a crucial component to egg production and laying. Hens that are too young to be breeding, are very small, live in too dry of an environment, or have been laying eggs excessively, thus depleting all her nutrition, may have difficulties with egg binding. Get an egg-bound bird to the vet immediately.

What About Bird Flu?

It is not a bad idea to have a quick discussion about bird flu, especially if you are worried about an outdoor aviary of finches. The bird flu, or influenza virus H5N1, has been a frequent topic of discussion. This particular strain of flu, which is highly dangerous to birds and may possibly be dangerous to humans as well, is being

Unexpected Eggs

If you have a pair of finches, chances are the hen will lay eggs. In fact, even if you have a hen without a mate, she may lay eggs (although these eggs will not hatch). If you have no room for more finches and don't want to breed, don't worry. Finches don't have to breed. Just avoid giving them nests and nesting material. Remove eggs as they are laid. The birds won't mind.

closely watched by scientists around the world. This strain of flu has proven deadly to some ducks and chickens, but it must mutate in order to be deadly to humans, and no one is sure if it will.

This virus is carried by wild birds, and though it has not yet made it into the United States, it is possible that it may be carried in by migrating birds. Do you need to worry about your finches and your family? Probably not. Chickens and ducks are highest at risk. If you and your finches are not exposed to poultry, everyone should be safe. If you are concerned, talk to your vet. Most likely, your favorite veterinarian will have a much more level-headed and fact-based view of the situation than what is portrayed by the media.

Fantastic Finches

Since finches are happier in pairs, even if you start with a single pair, you may find yourself thinking about breeding the cute little guys. Breeding finches for fun and for specific traits, as well as for showing them, can be a tremendous amount of fun. Just make sure that you have the resources to devote to your rapidly increasing flock.

Why breed?

Wouldn't it be fun to have some baby birds? After all, the more the merrier, right? If this is the only reason you're thinking of breeding finches, you should probably think a bit harder. Taking care of two finches takes some time and thought; taking care of a family of finches will be a lot more work.

If you have the space and the time to breed, it can be rewarding. Depending on which species you choose to breed, it can also be complicated and heartbreaking from time to time. If you are just getting started, chances are you will lose some chicks. Some of the most beautiful finches require special diets, perfect environments, and the right temperature and humidity to successfully rear babies. However, if you're convinced you want to breed finches, here are some things you should know.

A Single Pair or an Aviary?

It is probably best to start with a single pair unless you want to set up colony breeders. Zebra finches and society finches, for example, are happier breeding in groups, although both can breed in single pairs. If you have an aviary in the garden that you would just like to add birds to, you can always put in a group of colony breeders and let them do their thing. However, if you want to breed for particular characteristics or different species, you'll need to set them up individually.

Most breeders set up their pairs in individual cages and breed them at least once before putting them out into an aviary to breed. However, even if you breed in small cages, you'll need an aviary to release them into. Birds are in better physical condition and more likely to breed if they spend part of the year in an

Only the male red-cheeked cordon bleu finch has red cheeks. Other species may not be easy to sex.

aviary that allows them to really stretch their wings.

Distinguishing Pairs

It isn't always easy to tell male finches from females. In some finches, like zebra finches and Gouldian finches, the males have deeper colors and are sexually dimorphic, meaning they are easy to tell apart. Other finches are virtually impossible to sex visually. If they are social breeders, like society finches, you can purchase a group and see who pairs up. Otherwise, you'll need to depend on the breeder you buy finches from to sell you a pair. Buying a pair of finches that has already bred is a great way to ensure that you have a male and a female.

Pairing Up

Whichever two you put together, make certain that they are not related. You'll avoid the possibility of inbreeding. Once you've got a pair of finches set up, you'll want to make sure they are getting along and are likely to breed. If the two birds are new to one another, it's a good idea to put the male in the breeding cage first and let him claim it as his own for a couple of days before you put in the female. This way, it will be his territory, and she'll be more receptive than if the male were introduced into her territory.

Watch for signs of aggression from both birds. If one is chasing or attacking the other, they are not getting along. Watch for feather plucking, bleeding, and aggressive vocalizations. Keep a close eye on the birds; if there

Aggression

It is not funny when finches attack one another. You may think it looks cute to watch them square off and duke it out, but in the end, finch aggression can be deadly. Some males will defend their nest to the death, and that means keeping all other males away. There are certain species that have a tendency to be aggressive, and you should avoid mixing them with other birds when breeding. Keep in mind too that every finch is an individual and that some may be more aggressive than others.

is escalating aggression, one of the birds could be killed.

You will know that the pair of finches is getting along if the male is cooing or singing to the female. You should also see signs of mutual preening. This is different from plucking. It will look more like grooming. They should peacefully sit near one another, share food, and eventually mate.

A finch nesting box with kenaf fiber used as the nesting material.

Nesting

Whichever species of finch you decide to breed, be sure to do your homework and find out their preferred nesting habits. It isn't as simple as just putting two birds together and watching them become enamored with one another. They will need the right nesting site.

Types

One of the most common nests is a bamboo finch nest. It is an oval-shaped, covered-style nest with an opening on one side. Some birds may pull apart the bamboo for reconstructing the nest, but this actually encourages breeding. There are also covered nests made of grass and twigs or millet, and ones that hang from the top of the cage. There are uncovered baskets that are preferred by canaries. Ask around to other

breeders and see which type might best appeal to your birds.

Materials

Once you've chosen a nest style, you still need to supply nesting material. Some birds will build more intricate nests than others, but all need some materials with which to weave or line their nests. Find feathers, tissue paper, and dry grass. You can also supply your birds with coco fiber or burlap torn into single strands. Just be sure to avoid any material that the finches might get themselves tangled up in and become injured. Avoid anything that might be contaminated. Do not offer them string, cotton, lint, or pet hair.

Egg Laying

Once your finches have built a nest, the next step is laying eggs. Make sure

Breeding Diets

Finches that are breeding should have live insects supplemented in their diets, along with plenty of calcium and oil seeds. Some finches will eat live food only when rearing young and ignore it the rest of the year. Many breeders supply one or more of the following:

- Ant pupae
- Crickets
- Mealworms

- Silk Worms
- Wax worms
- White worms

Crickets

Mealworms

Silk Worms

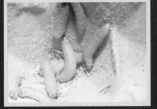

Wax Worms

White Worms

you supply your birds with plenty of cuttlebone for calcium, as well as plenty of fresh food and clean water. Laying eggs is stressful on the hen, and you should take care that she has everything she could possibly need.

When it comes time to lay eggs, you'll notice the hen spending a lot more time in the nest. When she begins to lay, she will lay one egg a day until she is done. Usually, the total is between one and six eggs. Then she'll start incubating them.

The male and female will take turns sitting on the eggs. After a few days, if the eggs are fertile, the embryo will begin to grow. If you are wondering if the eggs are fertile, you can gently remove them and "candle" them with a penlight or a small flashlight in a dark room. Eggs that have live embryos will have blood vessels running through them that you will be able to see as the light shines through the shell.

Take care when disturbing the parents on the nest. You don't want to do it frequently, but it's helpful if

the birds are used to you checking their nest from time to time. You will need to check eggs when you have breeding pairs.

Hatching

Depending on the species you are breeding, the eggs should hatch 12 to 15 days after the pair has started to incubate them. The chicks will break their way out into the world on their own slowly and ease themselves out of their egg shells. Some species of chicks are born with white or gray fuzz, and others are born completely naked, but they will gradually grow down and feathers. All chicks are completely dependent on their parents.

It is important that you do not disturb the nest for at least three or four days after the birds hatch. You may not want to disturb some species at all if you can tell they are still incubating. Finches, especially new parents, may abandon their babies if disturbed. Abandoned babies will die.

Sometimes, even if you don't disturb the nest, the parents will abandon their chicks. Some finches are terrible parents, and some need a couple of tries to figure it out. It is tough to lose baby finches, but unfortunately, it is part of breeding. If a baby is tossed from the nest or abandoned, and you have multiple breeding pairs, you can try slipping the baby under another hen. She may foster the baby. Society finches are often used as foster parents for finches that are difficult to breed, such as Gouldian finches. Once a pair has failed, clean out their nest and give

Old Enough to Breed?

Just because a hen is physically capable of laying an egg does not necessarily mean that she is old enough. Breeding your finches at too young of an age can be stressful and dangerous to the health of your birds. There is a good chance the chicks won't survive. Finches should be at least nine months old before you attempt to breed them.

Depending on the species, finch eggs hatch from 12 to 15 days after the pair starts incubation. Here are the early stages of a finch's life.

1 Society finch eggs in a nest box.

2 Egg beginning to hatch.

3 Two-day old society finch next to his unhatched siblings.

4 Seven-day old society finches with crops full of food.

them a chance to try again. Next time, they might get it right, but it's a good idea to have foster parents in mind in case they don't.

Growing Up

If the parents allow you to check on their chicks, you'll see their crops, pouches on the sides of their necks, filled like balloons. This is great. It means that the parents are feeding them and that they will probably keep growing—surprisingly fast.

Most finches will open their eyes when they are between five and eight days old. After their eyes open, their feathers will start to come in, and before you know it, they will be as big as their parents. The chicks will then begin to pop their heads out of the nest and check out the world. When they have all their flight feathers, they will begin to explore.

Young finches are especially fun. They are very tame during this time. They begin to feed themselves and explore their world fearlessly. This usually happens at about three weeks for most finches. In a couple of weeks, they will become less tame and begin their first molt. As their new feathers come in, they will begin to look like adults. You'll want to separate them from their parents at this point if they are in a smaller cage. In most species, the parents will naturally want to drive them away, and this aggression may become a problem.

The Expert Knows

Overbreeding

Finches are excellent breeders that will continue to raise chicks as long as the conditions are right. Since you provide a steady supply of excellent food, warmth, and a great breeding environment, your finches will breed all year if you let them. This is not a good idea, however. You can breed finches to death, and the hen will be the first to go. Laying eggs is hard on her little body. Be sure to give your finches a rest for several breeding cycles after they raise a nest of chicks. Pull out the nest so that they have nowhere to breed, and give them some time off.

Showing Finches

If you begin breeding birds and find yourself breeding for certain characteristics, such as color, you may find that showing finches is a natural progression. Finches breed and mature rapidly, which makes breeding for conformation (a perfect example of the species) or for particular color traits rewarding.

Why Show?

The first thing that you should know about showing finches is that there is no money in it. If you are thinking that you'll breed and show to make some extra cash, forget about it. You will spend a larger amount of money caring for and raising your finches than you will ever make by selling them. You may even have difficulty selling surplus stock. If you want to show finches, your motivation should be that you really want to win some of those little ribbons and be proud of your finches.

The Show Cage

If you are going to show finches, you must have the appropriate cage for exhibition. There are canary show cages, zebra finch show cages, and general finch show cages. All have specific dimensions and shapes. You will need to check with the National Finch and Softbill Society to get the right specs for the cage you need. It is important that the cage have no identifying marks or anything that would suggest whose bird is inside the cage. Also be sure to keep your show cage spotless and in good condition or you could lose points.

Cage Training

If you are going to show birds, it is important that your finches be comfortable and confident in the show cages. They should stay on the perch and not flutter around when the judge picks up the cage and moves it around. You can train your bird to enter the show cage by placing it, open, inside the aviary, with the finch's favorite food in it. This way,

you will not have to catch finches to get them into the show cage. After they enter the show cage voluntarily, spend some time putting the cage in areas of activity, taking care not to scare the finch but getting her used to the activity. A finch that is comfortable in its show cage will get higher marks when shown.

How Are the Birds Judged?

Finches are judged on characteristics that the National Finch and Softbill Society feel make up a perfect example of the species. This is not unlike the way judges evaluate purebred dog breeds in dog shows. However, your finch will be alone in a show cage where a judge can examine the various features of your finch up close. Finches are judged on conformation, condition, color, and marking as well as deportment and presentation. Conformation deals with the standards of the species head and body, wings and tail, and

To be a prizewinner at a finch show, your finch must be a perfect example of its type. This is a shaft-tail finch.

Hand Rearing

Hand rearing a finch is difficult, and most people who try fail. Finch chicks are so tiny that it is difficult to get the proper nutrition into them without causing them to aspirate (get food in the lungs). If you have a mentor who has been raising finches for a long time, you can try to learn from him or her, but it will still be a chancy endeavor. If you have chicks that have been abandoned by their parents, the best thing to do is have "foster parents" for them. You can slip chicks into a society finch nest and cross your fingers that the parents will feed them along with their own.

individual. The bird should be fully feathered, with every feather perfectly in place. The color and markings will be evaluated based on the standard colors for the species and perhaps the mutation of color for which your bird has been bred.

Last, the finch will be evaluated for deportment and presentation. Mostly, this is about how the bird behaves in the cage. The bird should be comfortable being on display and moving about. You may have to train the finch to perform well on show.

Since all birds are judged based on the standards for their species, if you wish to show finches, it's a good idea to contact the National Finch and Softbill Society to get the standards for the birds you are going to breed. It is a great idea to go to some bird shows and see the judging in action.

Banding and Record Keeping

If you are breeding finches for show or even just for certain characteristics, it will be critical that you band your birds for record keeping. This way, you can record band numbers and who the parents of the birds were. This will be an important method of repeating success and avoiding pairing that didn't work out.

Finches can be fitted with a numbered, closed band made of metal, which is slipped onto their leg at about 10 days old. The trick is for the band to easily slip on but for the feet and legs to be big enough that the band does not slip off. The band will be too large at first, but the finches will grow into it.

legs and feet. Finches will be expected to be correctly proportioned for their species and have no abnormalities.

Once the finch has been investigated for conformation, it will be examined for its condition and coloration. The condition of the bird involves evaluating the health of the

Do It Together

Showing finches is a wonderful activity to do with your children. You don't have to have a full aviary of finches to show; you can show the finches you breed from a single pair if you would like. Shows are a wonderful place for children to investigate the different kinds of finches and hear how other people care for their birds. Even better, how much fun it would be to take home one of those little ribbons!

cages. It is helpful to record the parent birds, the date the first egg is laid, and all other details of the breeding process. This is an excellent way to learn your finches' habits and natural cycles. In the future, you will be able to quickly note when something is amiss, and you will be able to easily track the lineage of all your birds.

There is a tremendous amount of information available in books, on the Internet, and through bird clubs regarding the breeding and showing of finches. This chapter gives you just a small percentage of the information you will need before you get started in either endeavor. Make sure that you do much more research before you begin to breed your first pair.

Fantasic Finches

The problem with fitting closed bands is that you must disturb the nest to do so.

Many breeders prefer to use split bands. Split bands are made of plastic and are multicolored as well as being numbered. These open and can be slipped onto a bird of any age. This is a good choice for a newly purchased bird that has not been banded. You can also use split bands to color-code the males and females of finch species that are not sexually dimorphic.

It is important to keep accurate records if you are going to breed. You can purchase special record cards or make your own and attach them to the

Note the band on this zebra finch. Banding helps breeders keep track of their finches' parentage.

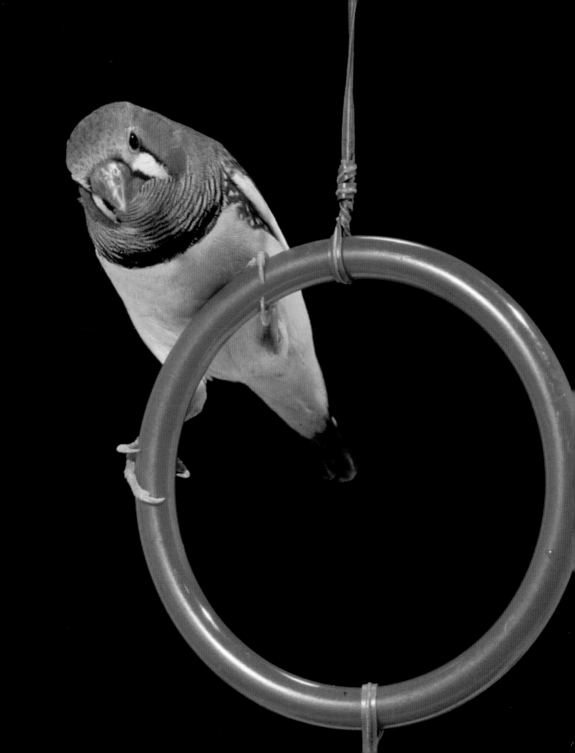

Chapter 7

The Wide World of
Finches

We've discussed a number of commonly kept finches, but every year, more and more species appear and become readily available to aviculturists. This chapter covers more of the finches that might catch your eye and find their way into your home. However, this is by no means a comprehensive list.

There is a tremendous variety of species of finches available in aviculture today. You should take care that the birds you purchase have been bred in captivity. Finches should not be taken from the wild, as many of them are extremely endangered. Finches that are close-banded have definitely been raised in a captive situation, but if they haven't been close-banded, make sure that you are buying your birds from a reputable breeder.

The finches that are listed in this chapter were chosen in order to give you a taste of the incredible variety of colors, sizes, and shapes of finches in aviculture. Some birds are prized for their songs, others for their spectacular coloration, and even others for their temperament and ease of breeding. You will have to make your own decision and perhaps investigate even more species to find the one that appeals the most to you and your situation.

European Goldfinch

The European goldfinch (*Carduelis carduelis britannica*) is one of the

The European goldfinch is a hardy species that is easy to breed.

Rare and Endangered

Many finches that are bred in captivity are endangered in the wild. This is one reason that you should not buy finches that were captured in the wild. Often, they are endangered because of a loss of habitat, which means it would be difficult to breed and release them. Gouldian finches are probably the most popular endangered finches, and it is likely there are less than 2,000 in the wild.

most popular birds in European aviculture. They are excellent breeders and talented singers, and are hardy and beautiful. They are native to Europe, northern Africa, and most of Asia and are found in grasslands, woodlands, orchards, parks, and even in gardens. Outside of the breeding season, they can be seen traveling in flocks as large as 100 birds.

The European goldfinch is about 5 inches (12.7 cm) long. The male and the female look similar and can be difficult to tell apart. The back of their head and nape are black, with a red forehead and throat. The cheeks, lower neck, and underside are white. The back is a dark chestnut color. The wings are black with yellow markings, and their tail is black and white.

These goldfinches have been bred in captivity for some time, and there are several mutations of their coloration. These include pastel, albino, pearl, and yellow. They can be a little bit aggressive but mix well with birds of similar size and temperament. However, there should be only one pair per aviary. They tend to lay three to five eggs, which hatch after 13 days of incubation. They are hardy birds and breed well if given proper space.

Green Singing Finch

The green singing finch (*Serinus mozambicus*) is also called a green singer or a yellow-fronted canary. Why it is called a "green" finch in the United States is a mystery, because the bird is mainly canary yellow. It is, however, a fantastic singer. The green singer is native to Africa, south of the Sahara Desert. Its habitat is open woodland and cultivated areas. It is a gregarious canary, except when breeding, and generally occurs in small flocks foraging on the ground for food. Their diet consists of grass, seeds, young shoots, and insects. They may also dine on nectar when breeding.

The green singer is 4.5 to 5 inches (11 to 12.7 cm) in length. The adult male has a greenish gray back and brown wings and tail. The chin, throat, underparts, and rump are yellow,

The green singing finch is closely related to the canary and similarly is a wonderful singer.

and the head is yellow with a gray crown and nape, and black eye stripe. The female is similar, but with duller underparts and a ring of indistinct black spots circling her throat.

Care must be taken in housing these birds in mixed aviaries with closely related species, as they will hybridize with other canaries. Males can be aggressive with one another, so only

Goldfinches

The European goldfinch is a popular bird in aviculture around the world, but they were having difficulties in the wild. In the 1970s, their numbers were in steep decline. It is thought that their population lowered because of the practice of spraying herbicides on weeds. Fewer weeds meant fewer seeds, and the finches had less food. However, findings by the British Trust for Ornithology show that they are making a comeback because of garden feeders.

one pair of this species should live in an aviary. They lay two to four eggs, which hatch after 18 days. They are hardy and can be difficult to breed but can be bred in a variety of cage sizes or aviaries.

Java Sparrow

Java sparrows—also called rice birds—(*Padda oryzivora*) are hardy, easy to breed, colorful birds that have an easy demeanor, making them great first finches. They have been popular for thousands of years, often depicted in ancient oriental art, no doubt because of their classy plumage. They are native to Indonesia, Java, and Bali but have been introduced to numerous other places. They prefer habitats of open country—such as grasslands, open woodlands, and cultivated lands—are highly gregarious, and travel in large flocks outside of breeding season, often feeding in rice paddies.

They are considered a large finch at 5.5 inches (14 cm) long. The male and female look nearly the same, with a black head, rump, tail, and wings. They have a bluish gray back and coverts.

Java sparrows are easy to breed. Several color mutations are available, including white.

Don't Mix

Although every bird is an individual, generally speaking the following birds should not be placed in a mixed-species aviary.

- Bar-breasted fire finch
- Crimson finch
- Cuban melodious finch
- Orange weaver
- Parson's finch
- Peter's twinspot
- Violet-eared waxbill

Parson's finch.

Their head is black, with white on the bottom half of the face. The throat and breast are a light bluish gray, and their underbelly is a pinkish gray.

The java sparrows are ready breeders and easily mixed in an aviary. However, their larger size can be intimidating to other smaller birds. They may be best mixed with larger or slightly more "pushy" finches. They breed best housed in groups, and prefer a larger cage at least 4 feet (1.2 m) long or, even better, a flight or aviary. They lay four to six eggs, which hatch after 14 days of incubation.

Orange-Cheeked Waxbill

The orange-cheeked waxbill (*Estrilda melpoda*) is an active little bird, with a flashy orange cheek patch. They are an attractive addition to a home or aviary but tend to have a nervous disposition, so they do better in a planted aviary, where they have room and ample area to hide. They are native to Africa from Senegal, Gambia, Cameroon, and northern Zaire to the western shore of Lake Albert, then southward from

Orange-cheeked waxbills are active but somewhat nervous finches.

Cameroon and northern Angola and across Katanga to northern Zimbabwe. They prefer to reside at the edge of cultivated land, along water in the tall grasses or in swamps. They live in small flocks that separate into pairs during the mating season.

Orange-cheeked waxbills are 4 inches (10 cm) long, with males and females having the same coloration. They have a red beak and orange cheek patches, which extend past their eyes. They are blue-gray on the top of their head, light gray under their chin, and light brown-gray on their chest. Their lower belly is a cream color, and their back and wings are dark brown. Their tail is black, with red coverts, and they have a yellow patch across their vent. This vent patch is darker on males but still difficult to distinguish.

These waxbills are fairly easy to breed, as long as they have large flights with plenty of cover. They are always timid birds, and disturbing their nests will cause them to abandon them. They also require a variety of live food in order to rear young successfully. They can be mixed with other finches

Team Players

Although every bird is an individual, these species generally mix well in an aviary of various species. Just make sure the birds have plenty of space and are of comparable size.

- Cordon bleu finches
- Gouldian finch
- Owl finch
- Parrot finches
- Society finch
- Spice finch
- Star finch
- Strawberry finch
- Waxbills

Tawny-breasted parrot finch.

but may become aggressive during breeding season and have to be removed. They lay four to six eggs, which hatch after approximately 14 days of incubation.

Orange Weaver

The orange weaver (*Euplectes orix franciscana*) is a brilliantly colored bird with orange and black feathers. The only thing more impressive than its coloring is its temperament. The orange weaver is a destructive and aggressive finch. They are native to northwestern and eastern Africa, where they prefer open savanna with tall thickets and trees.

The orange weaver is 4 to 5 inches (10 to 12.7 cm) long, with males and females having similar coloration except during the breeding season,

when the male molts into bright coloration. Out of season, the male is a mottled brownish tan, just like the female. From late summer to early winter, the male wears a brilliant orange in his collar, back of the neck, tail, and wings. The breast, abdomen, face, and top of the head become black. The females do not change color.

The orange weaver is a difficult bird to breed and is not a beginner's finch. The males become extremely aggressive during breeding season and will kill or die to remove another male from their territory. They are also dangerous to other species of finches. In the wild, the birds are polygamous, breeding harem style with one male to as many as females as he can defend in his territory. In a breeding situation, an aviary can have one male to as many as 10 females. The male will build the females their own elaborate nest. These birds can be kept in a smaller cage alone or with one male to one or two females but will be more likely to thrive in an aviary.

Owl Finch

The owl finch, or Bicheno finch (*Poephila bichenovii*), is an attractive and popular Australian finch with a face marked like an owl's. They are native to the steppes and savannas of northern, eastern, and interior Australia. They are sometimes seen in highly populated areas and are often found in parks and gardens. They are highly social and live in flocks of 4 to 20 individuals.

In the breeding season, the male orange weaver is brilliantly colored. At other times, he resembles the female.

Owl finches are generally hardy but are sensitive to cold temperatures.

The owl finches are 4 inches (10 cm) long, with males and females having the same coloration. They have a black forehead band that runs from above the eyes down the sides of the head and meets at the chin; the bird's face inside this band is white. The back of the head, neck, and back is pale brown with dark cross-barring, and the wings have a checkerboard pattern. The rump is black (or white depending on the subspecies), and the tail is a brownish black. The sides, throat, and belly are white, and there is another black band running under the chest.

The owl finch mixes well with other species and is prolific once it starts to breed. Males should be allowed to choose their own mates and will create a strong pair bond that should not be broken. They can be bred in cages, but in an aviary setting that is well planted, several pairs may nest in close proximity. The birds will lay three to six eggs, which will hatch after 12 days of incubation. Live food must be provided when the parents are rearing chicks. The owls are hardy but can be sensitive to temperature changes and should be kept in temperatures that do not drop lower than 68° to 72°F (20° to 22°C).

Red-Billed Fire Finch

The red-billed fire finch (*Lagonostica senegala*)—also called the Senegal fire finch—is brilliantly colored and a free breeder in captivity, making it an excellent addition to a mixed aviary. They are a widespread finch on the African continent south of the Sahara Desert. They prefer a natural habitat of bushy savannah or acacia scrub. Although they don't inhabit wetter regions, they are never too far from a water source.

They are 4 inches (10 cm) long, making them one of the smaller finches. The males and females are differently colored, making them easy to differentiate. The males are mostly

The male red-billed fire finch is mostly bright red in color and easy to tell apart from the female.

eye ring. The female has faint touches of red around the head, rump, and tail and is mostly brown, with darker brown flight feather shading to black toward the end. Her underbelly is lighter, and she has a yellow eye ring, although it isn't as obvious against the brown coloring.

deep red with small white spots on each side of the body and a light brown underbelly. The back and wings are brown, becoming darker toward the end of the flight feathers. They have dark brown eyes with a prominent yellow

The fire finches do fine in just about any size cage or aviary but will thrive in a large flight that has been planted. They are docile and will live in colonies with almost any other finches. They lay three to four eggs, which hatch at 12 to 13 days, and there is no need to remove the young after fledging. Although the fire finches are not singers, they have a wonderful demeanor and certainly add a touch of color to an aviary.

Color Variations

Some finch breeders breed their birds to preserve their wild characteristics. Others breed for interesting mutations in color. The more domestic species, like the zebra finches that have a long history in captivity, come in many different colors. Pied, fawn, cream, and white are common variations bred into many finches. Gouldian finches have striking color variations. They may be white breasted, blue backed, lilac breasted, or one of many other colorations.

Shaft-Tail Finch

The shaft-tail finch, or Heck's grass finch (*Poephila acuticauda*), is a larger Australian finch with elegant feathering and a clown's demeanor. They are native to northern Australia, where they inhabit grass and scrublands, but these birds are seen in parks and gardens on occasion.

The shaft-tail measures 6 to 7 inches (15.2 to 17.8 cm) long, but some of this length is the longer feathers in the tail. Males and females are similar in appearance and difficult to tell apart. The head is a soft gray color with black streaks around the eyes. Below the beak to the top of the chest is a black bib. The rest of the body is a soft gray color with a pink tinge, the underparts being slightly paler. The tail is black, with two long central shafts extending out. They have a broad black band on the body behind the legs, which is flanked with white.

Shaft-tail finches do well in cages or aviaries. They also do well in small colonies or mixed flights. They are active, and males frequently display to the females, making them interesting to watch. They are hardy and do well in cooler temperatures than most exotic finches. They are bred for several color morphs, including cream, white, and fawn. Females lay between five to seven eggs, which hatch in 14 days.

FAMILY-FRIENDLY TIP

Do It Together: Join a Club!

A great way to spend time with the family and make new friends is to join a club. There are many children and teenagers that are finch hobbyists. Not only will you get tips and tricks from other finch fanciers if you join a club, but you and your kids are certain to make new friends and increase the fun! Several finch clubs are listed in the Resources section of this book; you can find more on the web.

105

Male and female shaft-tail finches are difficult to tell apart.

Strawberry Finch

The strawberry finch, or red avadavat (*Amandava amandava*), is a brilliantly colored bird with an impressive song. They are an Asian species found naturally in India, China, Thailand, Java, Burma, Cambodia, Laos, Vietnam, and the Lesser Sunda Islands. They prefer open brush, sugar cane fields, open woodland, and grassy areas along waterways. When not in the breeding season, strawberry finches live in large flocks.

They are a smaller finch, 4 inches (10 cm) long. During the breeding season, the male molts in brilliant red plumage. The lores are black with a white stripe below the eye. Their head is a deep or scarlet red, and their back is brown with red-tipped feathers. The rump and upper tail coverts are red. The tail and midbelly are red, with white spots on the side. The wings are dark brown with white spots. Males

out of breeding plumage, and females, look similar but more muted with a brownish gray head. The throat and midbelly are yellowish, and the sides of the body are brownish gray.

Strawberry finches may be difficult to breed but are hardy, passive birds that mix well with other species. They can get aggressive during breeding season, especially with other red birds, but are generally fine. These birds seem to require exposure to enough sunlight and moisture in order to molt into their bright breeding plumage. It is best to have a single pair in an aviary. They lay four to seven eggs, which hatch after 11 to 14 days.

Tri-Colored Munia

The tri-colored munia (*Lonchura malacca*)—also called the tri-colored nun—is a popular species in captivity. Feral populations exist in many

During breeding season, male strawberry finches are red, but the rest of the year the sexes are difficult to distinguish.

different areas, including Puerto Rico. However, this species is only native to Asia, with most of the individuals imported to the US coming from Puerto Rico. The tri-colored munia has a light gray beak, a black head, and a

chestnut brown to mahogany body, wings, and tail. Some local varieties have a black belly and a yellow or orange tinge to the tail. The male has a beak that looks larger than the female's, but this indicator is not obvious enough to rely on for determining sex. Only the males sing, however.

Tri-colored munias generally get along well with other species of similar size.

Tri-colored munias are passive birds who get along fine with species of similar size. They prefer aviaries with tall grasses and reeds, where they will build nests. In the wild, they live in social groups and gather in rushes or reeds to roost at night. They are more likely to breed if allowed to choose their own mates. Their nails tend to become overgrown, so frequent nail trimming may be needed.

Tri-colored may hybridize with other finches of the mannikin family, so don't house them with other mannikins and munias. The average clutch size for this species is four to six eggs that will hatch after approximately 12 days. They appreciate live food when breeding. After the young fledge, they may continue to sleep in the nest for up to three weeks. They are fairly easy to breed.

Conclusion

Whichever birds you choose buy in order to enter the world of finches, make sure that you are completely prepared for the journey. Finches may be small and easier to take care of than some other birds, but they still deserve all the care and thought you can give them. The closer you can come to simulating what their lives would be like in the wild, the fewer problems you will have, and the healthier and happier your finches will be. Have your aviary or cage set up, your veterinarian chosen, and all the food, supplies, and extras that you might need already on hand. So now for the most important part: Enjoy! With the proper care and environment, these little feathered jewels will surely bring delight to your home.

Backyard Finches

Here are some wild finches you might see in your own backyard in the United States:

- American goldfinch
- Cassin's finch
- House finch
- Lesser goldfinch
- Purple finch
- Rosy finch

Resources

ORGANIZATIONS

American Federation of Aviculture
P.O.Box 7312
N. Kansas City, MO 64116
Telephone: (816) 421-3214
Fax: (816)421-3214
E-mail: afaoffice@aol.com
www.afabirds.org

Avicultural Society of America
PO Box 5516
Riverside, CA 92517-5516
Telephone: (951) 780-4102
Fax: (951) 789-9366
E-mail: info@asabirds.org
www.asabirds.org

Aviculture Society of the United Kingdom
Arcadia-The Mounts-East Allington-Totnes
Devon TQ9 7QJ
United Kingdom
E-mail: admin@avisoc.co.uk
www.avisoc.co.uk

National Finch and Softbill Society
Robert Mehl, Membership Director
11108 Hollowbrook Rd.
Owings Mills, MD 21117-1379
Phone: (410) 581-7955
E-mail: Robert.Mehl@verizon.net
www.nfss.org

EMERGENCY RESOURCES

ASPCA Animal Poison Control Center
Telephone: (888) 426-4435
E-mail: napcc@aspca.org (for non-emergency, general information only)
http://www.apcc.aspca.org

Bird Hotline
P.O. Box 1411
Sedona, AZ 86339-1411
E-mail: birdhotline@birdhotline.com
http:////www.birdhotline.com/

RESCUE AND ADOPTION ORGANIZATIONS

American Humane Association (AHA)
63 Inverness Drive East
Englewood, CO 80112
Telephone: (303) 792-9900
Fax: 792-5333
www.americanhumane.org

American Society for the Prevention of Cruelty to Animals (ASPCA)
424 E. 92nd Street
New York, NY 10128-6804
Phone: (212) 876-7700
http://www.aspca.org

Best Friends Animal Sanctuary
5001 Angel Canyon Road
Kanab, UT 84741-5001
Phone: (435) 644-2001
info@bestfriends.org
http://www.bestfriends.com/

Bird Placement Program
P.O. Box 347392
Parma, OH, 44134-7392
Phone: (330) 772-1627 or (216) 749-3643
www.avi-sci.com/bpp/

Caged Bird Rescue
911 Thomson Road
Pegram, TN 37143
Phone: (615) 646-3949

Exotic Bird Rescue Ring
http://www.neebs.org/birdresc.htm

Feathered Friends Adoption and Rescue Program
East Coast Headquarters
4751 Ecstasy Circle
Cocoa, FL, 32926
Phone: (407) 633-4744
West Coast Branch
Phone: (941) 764-6048
http://members.aol.com/_ht_a/
MAHorton/FFAP.html

The Fund for Animals
200 West 57th Street
New York, NY 10019
Phone: (212) 246-2096
fundinfo@fund.org

Northcoast Bird Adoption and Rehabilitation Center, Inc. (NBARC)
P.O. Box 367
Aurora, OH
Phone: (330) 425-9269 or (330) 562-6999
www.adoptabird.com

Royal Society for the Prevention of Cruelty to Animals (RSPCA)
Telephone: 0870 3335 999
Fax: 0870 7530 284
www.rspca.org.uk

Tucson Avian Rescue and Adoption (TARA)
Phone: (520) 531-9305 or (520) 322-9685
www.found-pets.org/tara.html

VETERINARY RESOURCES

Association of Avian Veterinarians
P.O. Box 811720
Boca Raton, FL 33481-1720
Telephone: (561) 393-8901
Fax: (561) 393-8902
E-mail: AAVCTRLOFC@aol.com
www.aav.org

INTERNET RESOURCES

Avian Network
www.aviannetwork.com/

Birds and Biology
home.wxs.nl/~erwinvr2/english.html

eFinch.com
www.efinch.com

Exotic Pet Vet.Net
www.exoticpetvet.net

Finch Aviary
www.finchaviary.com/

Finch Information Center
www.finchinfo.com/index.php

Finchworld
www.finchworld.com

MAGAZINES

Bird Talk
3 Burroughs
Irvine, CA 92618
Telephone: 949-855-8822
Fax: (949) 855-3045
http://www.birdtalkmagazine.com

Bird Times
7-L Dundas Circle
Greensboro, NC 27407
Telephone: (336) 292-4247
Fax: (336) 292-4272
E-mail: info@petpublishing.com
http://www.birdtimes.com

Good Bird
PO Box 684394
Austin, TX 78768
Telephone: 512-423-7734
Fax: (512) 236-0531
E-mail: info@goodbirdinc.com
www.goodbirdinc.com

Index

Boldfaced numbers indicate illustrations.

A

accessories, 25-31
adoption organizations, 108-109
aggression, 73, 87
aging, 7
air sac mites, 78
American goldfinch, 107
animal welfare groups, 108-109
ant baths, 61
aspergillosis, 80
Association of Avian Veterinarians, 76, 109
automatic feeding bowls, 27
avian flu, 82-83
avian gastric yeast, 81
avian veterinarians, 75-76
aviaries
    indoor, 23-24, **24**
    outdoor, 31-38, **32**, **36**

B

backyard finches, 107
bacterial infections, 81-82
banding, 94-95, **95**
bar-breasted finch, 100
bathing, 58-60
bath pans, 28, **28**, **37**, 59, **60**
beaks, 8-9, 78-79
beak trimming, 66
behavior. *See* temperament and behavior
Bengalese finch. *See* society finch
Bicheno finch. *See* owl finch
birdbaths, **37**, 59. *See also* bath pans
bird clubs, 105, 108
bird flu, 82-83
bird rooms, 24-25
birdseed, **44**, 45-48
bones, broken, 75
bowls, 27-28
breeding, 84-95
    age at, 90
    chicks, **91**, 92
    demands of, 86
    diets for, 89, **89**
    egg laying, 83, 88, 90
    hand rearing, 94
    hatching, 90-92, **91**
    nesting, 88
    overbreeding, 92
    pairing, 86-87
    record keeping, 94-95
    showing, 92-94, 95
breeding rooms, 37
broken bones, 75

C

cage covers, 28-29
cages, **20**, 20-23, **22**, 31, 74-75, 93.

See also housing
cage training for showing, 93
calcium, 54
canaries, 6, 11
candidiasis, 80-81
candling eggs, 90
carbohydrate, dietary, 43
Cassin's finch, 107
catching finches, 64-65
cats, 23
cereal seeds, 46
charcoal, 51
chemicals and chemical fumes, 23, 38, 71
chicks, **91**, 92
children
    bird clubs, 105
    feeding, 43
    finches as pets, 10, 21
    grooming, 60
    showing, 95
    sick finches, 76
cleaning, 38-39, 71
cleansers, 38
clubs and societies, 105, 108
coccidiosis, 79-80
colonies, 30-31, 86
color variations, 104
concrete perches, 25
cooked food, 51
cooking fumes, 23, 71
cordon bleu finch (*Uraeginthus bengalus*), 7, 15-16, **86**, 101
crickets, 52-53, **89**
crimson finch, 100
Cuban melodious finch, 100
cups, 27-28
cuttlebone, 54

D

deaths, 77, 78
diet and nutrition, 40-55
    amount to feed, 55
    birdseed, **44**, 45-48
    for breeding pairs, 89, **89**
    cooked food, 51
    eggs, **44**, 50-51
    food contamination, 70-71
    foods to avoid, 49
    fruits and vegetables, 48-50
    live food, 51-52
    molting and, 64
    nutritional requirements, 42-43
    pelleted diets, **44**, 44-45
    sprouted seeds, 50, **50**
    switching diets, 44-45
    vitamins and minerals, 42-43, 53-54, 62
    water, **54**, 54-55
    wild diets, 43-44
dishes, 27-28
dogs, 23, 38
domestic finches, 7

droppings, examination of, 72-75
dust baths, 61

E

ears, 9
egg binding, 82
egg laying, 83, 88, 90
eggs, as food, 44, 50-51
eggshells, 51
emergencies, 73, 74, 76
emergency resources, 108
endangered species, 98
escapes, 21, 22, 32, 34
Estrildidae, 6, 11
European goldfinch (*Carduelis carduelis britannica*), **98**, 98-99
exhibition cages, 20-21, 93
eyes, 8

F

fat, dietary, 43
feather care. *See* grooming
feather mites and lice, 77, 77-78
feather plucking, 62-63
feathers, 9, 58
feces, 72-75
feed bowls, 27-28
feeding. *See* diet and nutrition
feet, 9, 72, **73**
female finches, 13, 87
finches
    common types, 11-17
    general description, 6-10
    history of domestication, 5
first aid, 73, 74
flight cages, 33-34
flooring, for outdoor aviaries, 34
food contamination, 70-71
foods to avoid, 49
food storage, 39, 48
foot injuries, 9, 72, **73**
Fringillidae (true finches), 6, 11
fruits, 48-50
fungal infections, 80-81

G

gold-breasted waxbill, 7
goldfinches, **98**, 98-99, 107
Gouldian finch. *See* Lady Gouldian finch
greens, in diet, 48-49
green singers. *See* green singing finch
green singing finch (*Serinus mozambicus*), **99**, 99-100
grit, 53
grooming, 56-67
    ant baths, 61
    bathing, 58-60
    beak trimming, 66
    catching and handling, 64-65
    dust baths, 61

Finches

About the Author

Rebecca K. O'Connor has trained birds professionally at Disney's Animal Kingdom, Healsville Sanctuary in Australia, and many other places. She has been a falconer for over a decade and has experience working with a tremendous variety of animals, especially birds. She currently shares her California home with several birds and a Brittany.

Photo Credits

Cornel Achirei (courtesy of Shutterstock): 35 (bottom, far right); Samuel Acosta (courtesy of Shutterstock): 39; Steve Adamson (courtesy of Shutterstock): cover; R. D. Bartlett: 89 (bottom left); Bodhil1955 (courtesy of Shutterstock): 68; Katrina Brown (courtesy of Shutterstock): 35 (bottom, center left); Lance O. Brown (courtesy of Shutterstock): 37, 40; Karel Broz (courtesy of Shutterstock): 98; Michael Carlucci (courtesy of Shutterstock): 35 (top, center right); Tabatha Skye Campbell (courtesy of Shutterstock): 27; Bob Denelzen (courtesy of Shutterstock): 61; Susan Flashman (courtesy of Shutterstock): 34; Isabelle Francais: 24; Michael Gilroy: 10, 12, 18, 28, 30, 42, 48, 52, 55, 58, 67, 83, 84, 86, 96, 99, 100 (left), 105, 106, 107; Joanne Harris and Daniel Bubnich (courtesy of Shutterstock): 47, 56; Daniel Hixon (courtesy of Shutterstock): 26; Eric Ilasenko: 72; Eric Isselee (courtesy of Shutterstock): page number, 9, 17, 93; Bonnie Jay: 4; Jill Lang (courtesy of Shutterstock): 35 (bottom, center right); Horst Mayer: 8, 14, 16, 35 (extreme top), 45, 74, 91 (top right), 100 (right), 101 (both), 103; Vladimir Medarovic (courtesy of Shutterstock): 35 (top, center left); G. and C. Merker: 89 (top right); Alexei Novikov (courtesy of Shutterstock): 35 (bottom, far left); Prism 68 (courtesy of Shutterstock): 35 (top, far right); R. Gino Santa Maria (courtesy of Shutterstock): 35 (top, far left); John Tyson: 20, 22, 29, 44, 60, 63, 65, 95; Maleta Walls: 88, 89 (top center), 91 (top left and bottom); All other photos courtesy of T.F.H. Archives